THE BEST GIRLS IN THE WORLD

A History of the Sisters of St. Joseph of Rochester
in the Missions of Central Alabama, 1940-2020

Carol Cimino, SSJ, Ed.D.

NFB Publishing
Buffalo, New York

The Best Girls in the World: *A History of the Sisters of St. Joseph of Rochester*

in the Missions of Central Alabama, 1940-2020/Cimino- 1st Edition

ISBN: 978-1-953610-42-3

1.Title. 2. History. 3. Catholic Church. 4. Civil Rights Movement.
5. American Histoty.

NFB
<<<>>>
NFB Publishing/Amelia Press
119 Dorchester Road
Buffalo, New York 14213

For more information visit
Nfbpublishing.com

FOREWORD

THE MARKING OF THE eightieth anniversary of the arrival of the Sisters of St. Joseph of Rochester in Selma did not go off as planned. The pandemic, known as COVID -19 had shut down most of the country, and those Selmians who had been invited to the March 19, 2020 observance in Rochester, NY were barred from traveling. A few months later, in July of 2020, one of the most anticipated honored guests at that celebration, Representative John Lewis, passed away. Thus both the solemnity and the gaiety that should have been experienced at a celebratory gathering never happened.

But four score years of incredible presence of the pioneers, those five first Sisters-Sister Mary Ellen Dundon, Sister Catherine Charlotte Hyland, Sister Anastasia McCormick, Sister Francis de Sales Murphy, Sister Frances Marie Kehoe, and the almost one hundred Sisters that followed, should not go unnoticed. Ironically, the eightieth anniversary of the Sisters' presence coincides with the bicentennial of the incorporation of the city of Selma, and the need for an examination of this history and how it follows the trajectory of important events is a must.

I was honored to have been asked to write a history of the work and life of those many Sisters. I first visited Selma in December, 2019, and was appalled to note the continued poverty in an area that has been a witness to history and an eponymous chapter in the struggle for civil rights in the Deep South for the Black community. As I talked with the Sisters who are currently or were in Alabama, as well as long-term residents who worked with the Sisters at the school or at the hospital, or who were the recipients of the Sisters' largesse, I began to have a deeper appreciation for the better part of a century that has been the arena for Sisters' efforts to alleviate suffering and to bring attention to the ongoing plight of the people with whom they worked. This is not to be construed as a screed on the beneficence of white sisters for the Black community. Indeed, a mere quarter century after their arrival, events that had simmered all that time (think W.E.B. DuBois,

A. Philip Randolph, and Marcus Garvey)culminated in the Black community's autonomous risky actions calculated to secure their civil rights.

Most notably, the Sisters' witness to the events that took place in Selma as the struggle for civil rights boiled over must be observed. Their lived experience of this struggle was not acted out on the sidelines. They risked their own safety and even their lives before, during, and after the events that have defined "Selma" and made it synonymous with the civil rights movement. It was not the flash and noise of historic events that defined their work; it was the daily effort to get to know the people of Selma and its environs, and the small but significant gestures that the Sisters offered to make so many lives better, and even more important, to let them know that somebody cared.

Although the Selma mission was begun and has been sustained by the Society of St. Edmund priests and brothers, I wanted to focus on the Sisters; hence there are extensive quotes and excerpts from interviews, correspondence, and records from the Sisters of St. Joseph archives. Here, I would like to acknowledge the assistance of the archivist for the Sisters of St. Joseph of Rochester, Kathleen Urbanic, a true professional, a generous assistant and a patient complier of requests for documents. The COVID-inspired lockdown at the Motherhouse made research especially tricky, but, thankfully, did not dampen the ingenuity of Kathleen in transmitting material.

Special mention is due to the Edmundite Mission and the Conrad Hilton Foundation grant for helping to support this effort and to Susan Raymond who secured funds for the publication of this book.

The Sisters whom I interviewed and recorded were most generous. Almost to a person they retrieved mementoes, photos, and records of their tenure in Alabama. They are quoted verbatim here, and their words come from a profound and unique experience in their religious lives. Interviews with the residents of Selma, during my second visit to Selma in February of 2021 were also recorded, and, though at times they are conflated for brevity, they are faithfully related here.

Of note is the fact that the use of the words "colored" and "Negro" are direct quotes from primary sources and were used respectfully, in their time, to refer to Black persons.

If anything, my intent here is to honor the intrepidity, courage, vision, and just plain hard work of the Sisters of St. Joseph who so generously gave of their energy and comfort. If conditions in Selma, Pine Apple, Vredenburgh and other areas in central Alabama are still dire, it is not because the Sisters were not successful. No one can measure the amount of empathy, comfort, care, and love that Sisters of St. Joseph have so prodigally applied. But every one whose life has been touched by the Sisters would agree that they are still "the best girls in the world."

Author's Note
The words "colored" and "Negro" are used throughout the book. They are only used when quoting sources from earlier eras before they were recognized as unacceptable.

THESE HERE ARE THE BEST GIRLS IN THE WORLD

As the crow flies, it is exactly 1,016 miles from Rochester, New York to Selma, Alabama. It may as well be a million miles. Selma is to Rochester as Mars is to Earth; where Upstate New York is verdant, Selma boasts red clay. Where Rochester consists of miles of arterial highways, Selma has no direct highway to any other major city in Alabama. Where Rochester shows off whole neighborhoods of neatly kept homes, Selma has an abundance of boarded- up or totally abandoned houses. To the five Sisters of St. Joseph of Rochester who arrived, after an arduous journey, in Montgomery, Alabama on September 19, 1940, it may as well have been Mars.

The very name of Selma, Alabama stirs up emotions, memories, and opinions. In many ways, Selma represents the ugly heritage of blatant racism and the emergence of the Black community from its horrible burdens. Indeed, the motto of present-day Selma is "From Civil War to Civil Rights and Beyond". Leaders and residents of Selma have been vilified, and have become the personification of all that was wrong with the Deep South during the days of juridical segregation. But, although the leaders of Selma, most notably its long-tenured Sheriff Jim Clark, have been portrayed as the devil incarnate, one must also note that there have always been decent persons, too. Selma has suffered for all the sins of the South, and there were many, but the current inhabitants are also proud of their unique heritage.

Five Sisters of St. Joseph: Sister Frances Marie Kehoe, Sister Mary Ellen Dundon, Sister Catherine Charlotte Hyland, Sister Anastasia McCormick, and Sister Francis de Sales Murphy, were blessed and missioned to work with the priests of the Society of St. Edmund in Selma, Alabama on Sunday, September 15, 1940.

Why these five were chosen to begin this mission can be ascertained by an examination of their backgrounds. One can imagine Mother Rose Miriam Smyth combing the list of Sisters and their qualifications in order to make her decision as to whom to send.

Sister Frances Marie Kehoe was anointed the superior of this first group of Sisters. She was 53 years old when she went to Selma, and had worked as a teacher in the Rochester Diocesan schools, as well as at St. Mary's Orphanage. She was also a member of the team that opened Holy Childhood School, an educational institution for children with special needs. The variety of the ministries in which she served prior to her arrival in Selma provided the resiliency and skills that she would need in this new place. Upon her departure from Selma in 1946, she took up teaching again, and worked in various schools into her nineties. She died in March, 1984.

Sister Mary Ellen Dundon was originally from Buffalo, NY. She was 21 years old when she was sent to Selma, having entered the Sisters of St. Joseph only two years prior to her assignment in Alabama. She was only in Selma for a year, doing clerical work in the parish of St. Elizabeth's. Upon her return to Rochester in 1941, she became a teacher, and, eventually, a school administrator, known for her pursuit of educational innovation. She died on January 28, 1971 at the age of 52 after a long illness.

Sister Catherine Charlotte Hyland was born in Penn Yan, New York in 1882, and was 58 years old when she went to Selma. While she had been a teacher for six years, she went on to do domestic work prior to her assignment in Alabama. She was, in all likelihood, intended to be the housekeeper and cook for the Sisters. She spent two years in Selma, returning to Rochester in 1942 to supervise one of the dormitories at Nazareth College. Sister Catherine Charlotte died on November 5, 1958.

Sister Anastasia McCormick was 58 years old when Mother Rose Miriam Smyth tapped her to help begin the work in Selma. A brilliant nursing student at St Joseph's Hospital in Elmira, New York, she earned 100% on every state board exam for which she sat. Since the creation of a hospital was part of the long -range plan of the Edmundites, she was a natural choice for the mission, and served there for four years. Upon her return to Rochester in 1944, she resumed nursing duties in various ministries of the Sisters of St. Joseph. She passed away on May 1, 1976.

Sister Francis de Sales Murphy was 35 years old when she stepped off the train in September, 1940 with the other Sisters. She had been a teacher in various Rochester Catholic schools and was, no doubt, intended to partner with Sister Frances Marie to open a school in Selma. However, for unknown reasons, she left Selma only two months after she arrived and resumed her teaching career in Rochester.

Due to the early departure of Sister Francis de Sales Murphy, her successor should be counted among the original Sisters. Sister Francis David Backman arrived on November 15, 1940. At age 28, she already had an impressive record as an elementary school teacher in the Diocese of Rochester. Sister Francis David spent fourteen years helping to found and staff St. Elizabeth's School in Selma. So valued would her contributions to the Edmundite Missions be that, in 1990, she received an honorary Doctor of Humane Letters degree from the Edmundites' college, St. Michael's, in Winooski, Vermont, for "typifying the missionary spirit shown by the Sisters of St. Joseph of Rochester in their Alabama ministries" (Sisters of St. Joseph press release, May 3, 1990). Sister Francis David returned to Rochester in 1954, taught for two years, and then returned to Selma in 1956, spending the next six years as principal and seventh and eighth grade teacher at St. Elizabeth's School. She died on June 7, 1999.

THE sermon at the missioning ceremony, on September 15, 1940, was delivered by the Reverend Martin Watley, Director of the Propagation of the Faith from Syracuse, New York. He shared his vision of a "magnificent harvest" from the work of the Sisters. In other words, the purpose of the sisters' presence in the Deep South was the cultivation of souls for the Catholic Church, as well as the support of those Black people who were Catholic, but were a distinct minority in the Protestant South.

Our first Sunday in Selma and how shall I describe our sensations as we found ourselves the only white people in a congregation of about eighty. Even the altar boys were [B]lack and non-Catholics. (Letter from Sister Frances Marie Kehoe to Mother Rose Miriam Smyth, September 22, 1940)

But they must have made a great impression that first Sunday, as, at a reception to welcome these unseasoned Northerners, Jeremiah Dillard, at 84 the oldest parishioner of St. Elizabeth's parish, remarked: "These are the best girls in the world!"

Father Casey, then the priest in charge of the Alabama mission, in a letter to Father Randall of the Propagation of the Faith, in the summer of 1939 opined that "the ordinary procedure in the Colored Missions (sic) here in the South...is to bring Sisters to the Mission and open a school." But first the Sisters set about to adjust to the tremendously different milieu into which they had been deposited. The oppressive heat and humidity (and they wore the traditional, wool serge all-encompassing black habit of seventeenth century France) conspired to sap the strength from the Sisters. The foreign culture of Southern Black Americans, the suspicion of Roman Catholics by the non-Catholic clergy and the local Ku Klux Klan, the grinding poverty and lack of opportunity for Black people, descendants of slaves, and the dictates of maintaining a traditional religious regimen were daunting challenges. With their founder, Father Medaille's strictures in mind, they set out to do "everything of which a woman is capable." This is their story.

THE INVITATION TO THE SISTERS BY THE EDMUNDITES

AT 6:30 IN THE morning of Thursday, September 19, 1940, two days after the Sisters embarked on their journey from Rochester, New York, they arrived in Montgomery, Alabama. Father Casey, their contact with the Edmundite Fathers, was there to meet them. After two long days on a train, one would imagine the weariness of these five women, who, in all probability, just wanted a chance to rest and get their bearings. Instead, a brief tour of central Alabama would have to be endured before they could relax.

Their first impression can be summed up on the report to the Motherhouse on September 22, 1940:

> [Father Casey] drove us immediately to St. Margaret's Church, where he said Mass...After breakfast at the rectory, we drove out to St. Jude's where we met Father Purcell and toured his school. While still in Montgomery we visited St. John's School, run by Mother Catherine Drexel's nuns. About an hour's drive brought us to Selma at our own front door. Our first visit was to the pretty little chapel, where Our Lord was waiting to welcome us. Then we went to the dining room where the first course of our dinner was already on the table.

The Sisters had arrived.

Their arrival was presaged by two serendipitous encounters, in the summer of 1939; the first between Father John Randall, director of the Rochester office of the Propagation of the Faith, and Father Francis Casey, a member of the Society of St. Edmund, and director of their missions. The second was a more profound one between Father Randall and the head of the Sisters of St. Joseph of Rochester, Mother Rose Miriam Smyth.

The Society of St. Edmund had been founded in 1843 in Pontigny, France, some two hundred years after the founding of the Sisters of St. Joseph in LePuy, France. Members of the Society fled to North America in 1889, due to religious intolerance in France. In 1937, the Society found its métier in the establishment of a mission in Alabama dedicated to helping Black Americans.

The Edmundites had begun their mission in Selma, Alabama in 1937, with a parish named St. Elizabeth's. Father Casey, responsible for the mission's sustenance, was seeking financial support and "if he knew any Sisters who might come to help" from the Propagation of the Faith in Rochester. In July, Father Randall happened to be in Elmira, New York and dropped by St. Joseph Hospital to congratulate the newly-elected Mother Rose Miriam Smyth. The conversation turned to Mother Rose Miriam's desire to found a mission in the South for "the colored."

Mother Rose Miriam Smyth was an intellectual, studying and mastering a Russian language course in her eighties, and she presided over the congregation through the Great Depression and World War II (1939-1951), while expanding the areas in which the Sisters of St. Joseph provided a caring presence to the people of Rochester and its environs.

Mother Rose Miriam had held the plight of the "colored people" in her heart for quite some time. Every Sunday, she went to the facilities of the St. Peter Claver Society, on Rome Street in Rochester, where she taught catechism to the Black children. Upon the founding of Nazareth College in 1924 (while she served on the leadership council of the Sisters of St. Joseph), she encouraged the first students of that college to volunteer their efforts at the Charles Settlement House, originally founded to aid newly-arrived immigrants, and eventually becoming a place of solace for the Black community of Rochester. The invitation forwarded by Father Randall was an answer to prayer.

The very thought of sending Sisters was a true leap of faith. Mother Rose Miriam had no idea of the situation in Selma, and the Edmundite Fathers had made it clear that they had no money to pay the Sisters, nor the means of supporting them, and not even a photograph to offer. In an attempt to get the "lay of the land", Mother Rose Miriam requested that Father Casey send some pictures. On March 14, 1940, he replied: "There is not, at the minute, a single snapshot of anything down here available..." But he promised to send some as yet undeveloped prints as soon as possible, and, in an aside, he mentioned that the Edmundites were to open a mission soon in

North Carolina: might there be some interest there?

Although the Congregation of the Sisters of St. Joseph of Rochester was, in 1940, a Diocesan order, that is, subject to the authority of the local Bishop, church law allowed that the Sisters might work outside the diocese at the request of another bishop. When Bishop Thomas J. Toolen, Bishop of Mobile, Alabama, made that request, the newly appointed Bishop of Rochester, James E. Kearney, gave his consent.

As mentioned above, the primary purpose for bringing Sisters to the Selma mission was the evangelization of Black people, and the support of Black Catholics in the South. This would, eventually, be carried out by the establishment of a Catholic school, and, later, a hospital. The Sisters of St. Joseph of Rochester were known as excellent educators in the Diocese of Rochester, staffing, by 1940, 56 elementary schools and three high schools. (Sisters of St. Joseph of Rochester, 1950). However, much groundwork had to be laid before the Sisters could open either a school or a hospital, and the Sisters set about assessing the needs of the people right away.

FUNDING THE MISSION

AS HAS BEEN NOTED above, the mission at St. Elizabeth's parish was begun in 1937, when the Society of St. Edmund was asked to send some priests to provide spiritual and corporal works of mercy to Selma's Black Catholics. In order to maintain and expand that mission to include education and health care, the Edmundites, as did many of the clergy, looked to attract a community of Sisters. As Coburn and (1999) point out:

> *The sisters' role in parish education was extensive. They served as teachers, principals, fund donors and fund-raisers, sponsors for religious organizations, choir directors, coaches, and social workers in a hierarchical Church. (pp.129, 130).*

Sisters received no salary for their labors during the nineteenth and early twentieth centuries and it was acknowledged by Father Casey that the Edmundites had no funds to pay a salary to the Sisters. They would, however, see to it that the Sisters had basic necessities, and would do as much as they could to make the Sisters safe and comfortable. And so, in July and August, 1940, a project to fund the new missionary effort in Selma was undertaken with several events, the most notable a series of concerts, "Opera Under the Stars", in Rochester's Highland Park. This effort was spearheaded by the Alumnae Association of Nazareth Academy, an all-girls' high school founded by the Sisters in 1871, whose contributions would continue for many years. The noted Rochester Philharmonic conductor, Jose Iturbe, no less, was scheduled to conduct a series of three classical music performances and balletic demonstrations for the cause of the Selma mission. These concerts were so successful that a fourth was scheduled and the *Rochester Catholic Courier-Journal* of August 8, 1940 gushed that "the concerts are not only a bow in the direction of good music, but will be a direct benefit for the Selma, Alabama mission of the Sisters of St. Joseph."

In addition to the concerts, various parishes were tapped to contribute to the cause, and the families of Sisters themselves were encouraged to share their generosity. The cousin of Sister Angelita made a pledge of the princely sum of $500 (probably "$50,000 in 2021 value) to the Sisters' chapel. Sister Angelita reported to Mother Rose Miriam this generous windfall: " I am so delighted about this gift that I cannot write evenly. My hand is shaking like a leaf."

How satisfied Mother Rose Miriam must have been reviewing the faith and generosity of the people of the Diocese of Rochester. One may imagine her awe at receiving checks for $5.00 that represented a real sacrifice for the donor, especially in 1940 when the Great Depression was still felt. At last, several thousand dollars had been raised, and the actual commendation of the first missionaries would be undertaken, along with plans for their travel to the South.

The coordination of the support of the Sisters, from the outset, was done by Father Randall, because he was the head of the Propagation for the Faith in Rochester. Designated parishes in the Diocese of Rochester, and the forgiveness of salaries from the Sisters of St. Joseph made the endeavor financially viable. It should come as no surprise that the costs of maintaining the life of the Sisters would rise; after all, they were constantly bringing food and other supplies to the people whom they visited, and driving them to medical appointments. In addition, the annals reveal that the Edmundites supplied both a cook and a laundress for the Sisters. The state of finances, especially the support of the Sisters, seems to have been the constant topic on the mind of Father Casey, and his successor, Father Lambert. In a letter to Sister Vincentine, then the superior of the Sisters in Selma, Father Randall lamented:

> It was with some alarm that I observed your statement: 'the budget for four sisters was $5500'(worth $102,764 in 2020 dollars). I would very much appreciate, if you care to give it, a more itemized statement of these expenses; likewise the sources from which the money was contributed, for I doubt that in any one year such an amount passed through this office. Frankly, it seems to me extremely high. If it includes expenses other than living, then I could see ample justification, but if it applies only to living essentials, it seems to me extremely out of line.

I do think, sister, that inasmuch as this office (Propagation of the Faith in Rochester) has provided the bulk of your support, we should be entitled to have more information as to the way it was used. (Letter from Father John Randall to Sister Vincentine, October 11, 1946).

Matters seemed to need clarification when, on December 4, 1946, Father Lambert attempted to clarify the issue of finances:

To the present time all agreements and promises have been reached or given orally. To my mind it has resulted in much confusion. I wish to insist on one request, viz., the existence of a written agreement or policy concerning your community in regards to your Selma mission...Mother, I dislike floundering around in the dark as much as you do; it always ends in misunderstanding.

He went on effusively lauding the Sisters and their effort in the mission, and noted, "There is not a single complaint about the Sisters either considered collectively or individually. Their zeal and charity is [sic] ever a source of inspiration." (Letter from Father Lambert to Mother Rose Miriam, December 4, 1946).

Although such copy of a written agreement cannot, to this day, be found, perhaps the matter of financing the mission was eventually settled, as Father John Randall wrote to Sister Vincentine on September 24, 1947, nine months after Father Lambert had requested a written agreement:

It was a pleasure to have your letter of September 12th(1947) and I hasten first to explain what we mean by the Missionary Plan of Cooperation. This Plan...obligates each parish (in the Diocese of Rochester) to accept either a foreign or a home mission and... take up a collection for a particular need. In our effort to support the missions in Selma we have reserved a group of parishes each year for this purpose...Have I ever mentioned that this money is to be used for your needs in maintaining the convent? The enclosed check from Our Lady of Victory completes the group returns for this year.

Even so, Father Lambert lamented the rising costs, even as more Sisters were sent to Selma to operate the school and the hospital.

We recognize the fact that living costs have been rising constant-
ly, but we are also wondering why the Sisters' usual source of sup-
port is not meeting this condition...Again, we prefer to respectfully
ask for a written contract or agreement. At that time the question
of salary for both the hospital and school Sisters will be generously
settled. (Father Lambert to Mother Rose Miriam, September 16,
1948).

He went on to write:

Please understand that we are not adverse (sic) to helping the
Sisters financially. Far from it. However, what emergency will arise
six months or a year from now? Whatever arrangement would ob-
tain presently may not work out satisfactorily for the future.(Fa-
ther Lambert to Mother Rose Miriam, September 16, 1948).

It is important to note that, even with the constant worry of finances,
the Edmundite Fathers chose faith over finances. The fact that the mission
is thriving after over 80 years is a testimony to their dedication to the mission and their belief that, if it was God's will that the mission survive, God
would have a hand in insuring that.

The Edmundite priests, solicitous for the safety of the Sisters provided
a dog,. There are several mentions of the dog's lack of manners, as he once
got onto the waiting dinner table and proceeded to help himself. At other
times he chewed up Sisters' clothing, or test papers awaiting correction,
perhaps giving rise to the "dog ate my homework" tradition. On September
20, 1940, the day after the Sisters' arrival, Sister Frances Marie wrote: "Penny Murphy [as the dog was known], got into our improvised icebox on the
drain board and ate our butter." In any case, Penny Murphy was summarily
dispatched to Anniston, Alabama on December 12, 1940. As the annals put
it, "Thereby ends the brief but exciting period of his life in the convent."

Four days after the butter theft, Sister Frances Marie recounted:

The insects seem to be holding the upper hand today. When I
brought the mail over I found everyone running around with tea-
kettles. Sister Anastasia was quite perturbed about maggots in the
backyard. Sister Catherine Charlotte was working on ants in the
dining room, Sister Francis de Sales staunchly held off the advanc-

ing ants on the threshold. A truce was called in time for us to get a
little rest before the next day (September 24, 1940).

Assuredly, the arrival of these Sisters, bizarre shapes with their seven-teenth century European wool serge habits and Northern ways, presented a real challenge to that vaunted Southern hospitality. One of the Edmundites wrote: "Many of the children and some of the grownups had never seen a nun. "

Father Casey, in a letter to Father Randall prior to the Sisters' arrival, re-sponded to Father Randall's query regarding the Sisters' black serge habits and their place in the hot and humid Southland:

There are many reasons, excellent ones, why a nun garbed in
Secular-like uniform has a decided advantage over those in reli-
gious habits...Today I answer without hesitation that the religious
habit with all its handicaps is a decided advantage. The reason
is that the Southerners, Catholics and non-Catholics, black and
white, have an admiration for nuns which is truly profound. ...To
them, however, a sister and a religious habit go together...It seems
to me, a grievous mistake in our work for souls to overlook the
tremendous amount of 'good will' which we have at our disposal in
the religious habit of a sister (Letter from Father Casey to Father
Randall July 29, 1939).

By the 1960s, the Sisters would be able to wear a white habit, made of a lighter material; in fact, in 1964 the Sisters of St. Joseph began a mission in Brazil and wore the white "missionary habit. By the 1970s, Sisters could wear a gray skirt and veil with a white blouse, and the end of the 1970s meant that Sisters could dress in "secular garb."

In many ways, the arrival of the Sisters with their traditions mirrored the arrival of Sisters from various communities in the nineteenth centu-ry. Where the founders and foundresses of those congregations bade their members, while in Europe, to assume the habitual clothing of European widows so that they would blend in with the populace and be able to go about their ministry, their appearance in the New World had just the op-posite effect.

The Sisters also transferred their daily and weekly horarium from Rochester to Selma. The annals reveal that, although the climate and the living conditions might sap the strength out of them, nonetheless, Sundays saw them attending three Masses in the morning, catechizing in the afternoon, attending Benediction and the rosary, and, in the evening, running the social gatherings for the youngsters.

Even before the Sisters' arrival, Father Casey had some concerns regarding the daily schedule that would be followed by the Sisters and wrote, not to Mother Rose Miriam, but to Father John Randall:

> There is no reason why there should be any difficulty about this point: It concerns the hours of Community devotions and exercises as set by the Rule. Nuns engaged to work down here should be allowed to so arrange their community exercises that they do not interfere with the work they have to do, and vice-versa (Letter from Father Francis Casey to Father John Randall, July 29, 1939).

This would, eventually, become a bone of contention for the Sisters; as their duties gradually increased, the grueling schedule would become onerous to the point of straining the relationship between the Sisters and the Edmundite Fathers.

A footnote to the Sisters' presence is worth noting. Christine Saldanha, a lay woman who had been with the Benedictines in England, arrived from London in 1940, at the behest of Mobile, Alabama Bishop Thomas Toolen,. She had contacted him after reading an article on the need for missionaries in the South. Although World War II was a year old in Europe, and travel across the Atlantic treacherous, Christine traveled to the United States to work in the Southern missions. She wrote of her departure:

> Thus it came about that I set sail on a bleak November morning from Tilbury, the Port of London. Just before I bade the last good-bye, someone said, 'whatever you do, don't go and enter a convent over there!' I can hear my answer now...'As if I would"(Memoir of Sister Christine Francis Saldanha, c. 1962).

While she worked with the Edmundite Fathers in Selma, Christine lived with the Sisters of Mercy at Assumption Convent. Eventually, she wrote to Bishop Toolen that she had decided to enter religious life:

> ...[M]y next difficulty was the choice of an order. I was living

with and loved the Sisters of Mercy, but they were gradually re-
linquishing their colored missions...Race prejudice is very strong.
September 19, 1940 saw the installation of the Sisters of St. Joseph
from Rochester in their modest quarters in the colored section. ...
[A]bout two weeks later, Father Casey suggested I take a 'vacation'
in Rochester. ...I knew that I loved Rochester. I [traveled to other
places in the North]...but ...the Sisters of St. Joseph of Rochester
had stolen my heart. I wanted to be a Sister of St. Joseph and return
to the South to work again among God's 'least of little ones' (Mem-
oir of Sister Christine Francis, c. 1962).

Sister Christine Francis never returned to the South, but taught English
and science at Nazareth Academy for many years, and then in the Biology
Department at Nazareth College; she died in 1973. Hers is an incredible
journey, and a testament to the witness of the Sisters who labored in Selma.

As the years passed, the daily toll on the Sisters became more onerous;
they worked all day and then worked all night. Their weekends meant
more work and, upon the departure of Sister Frances Marie, the first superior, the arrival of her replacement, Sister Vincentine, in September, 1945
brought a new perspective. A year into her tenure, the Sisters hosted a visit
from Sister Helene Garvin, a member of the Council of the Sisters of St.
Joseph. Apparently, she met with Father Lambert at the conclusion of her
visit and aired several issues with relation to the Sisters' work burden. Father Lambert subsequently wrote to Mother Rose Miriam to let her know
about the contentious conversation he had had with Sister Helene:

Our conversation dealt with generalities, but Sister Helene gave
enough hints to impress me that something was wrong. My first
and lasting reaction was that Sister had a chip on her shoulder
and spoiling for a fight (at least one of your Sisters here received
the same impression).... Basically, her [complaints] can be resolved
to the following: the Fathers of St. Edmund have been [overwork-
ing] the Sisters of St. Joseph in the Selma Mission... That is serious
charge. (Letter of Father Lambert to Mother Rose Miriam, Decem-
ber 4, 1946).

Father Lambert eventually relieved the Sisters of the management of the clothes room, advised them that they would no longer do catechetical work or home visits, and that they would have a confessor that was not an Edmundite.

In the letter, where Father Lambert lamented the Congregation's refusal to send more Sisters to Selma to do the work, he pointed out that he hoped that relieving the Sisters of the above-mentioned duties would encourage more Sisters to come to Selma. His letter reveals the admiration he had for the Sisters' dedication to the work, and the Edmundites' desire to expand that work.

In the same letter he noted:

> I know, dear Mother, that you will be happy to learn there is not a single complaint about the Sisters.. Their zeal and charity is ever a source of inspiration.

Father Lambert wrote, in 1949, that the Sisters' support would be "made up from the hospital 'donated services', and, in the same letter importuned Mother Rose Miriam to allow the Sisters added work:

> During our discussion you explained how it was impossible for you to ever contemplate allowing your Sisters to do tubercular(sic) nursing and night supervisory work at the hospital. You did give me to understand, on the other hand, that catechetical and instruction work is within the program of the teaching Sisters. (Letter to Mother Rose Miriam, June 20, 1949.

Thus the nursing Sisters' duties were eliminated, and the teachings Sisters' duties were enlarged.

If the Sisters thought that the matter of their doing catechizing was settled, they were mistaken. In 1961, Sister Francis David Backman wrote to Mother Helene Garvin, who succeeded as General Superior Mother Rose Miriam Smyth:

> Father Ziter has just asked that the Sisters teach Religion to the high school students on Sunday evenings from 7:30 to 8:30. It would be the freshmen and sophomores, boys and girls. They are to have a social hour before followed by the class. Should we do it?

She further clarified:

> *I have said no to the request on other occasions so that Father feels I am uncooperative. There are other priests, two of whom have few duties, and brothers, too. Because it comes up again and since the new horarium, I would like your opinion (Letter from Sr. Francis David to Mother Helene February 5, 1961).*

Of course, it had been that same Sister, now Mother Helene, who, in 1945, had importuned Father Casey to relieve the Sisters of this task. One may also surmise that the Sisters' energy and initiative only encouraged the priests to expect more and more of them. In the end, the Sisters did not have to do the catechizing. On November 5, 1961, two Trinitarian Sisters arrived "to do CCD." (Archives)

In more ways than one, the Sisters carried the Church Militant of the 1940s with them to their new home. The Baptist ministers were initially suspicious of the Sisters, fearing that they would entice souls over to the Catholic Church. But an entry into the annals of November 28, 1940 reported that the Sisters took the first steps towards reconciliation:

> *Sisters Frances Marie and Francis David went over to the Baptist Church next door [to the convent] to look over the building. Dr. Jemison, the preacher, very graciously showed them through the building from top to bottom.*

This was a shrewd move, an offering of a symbiotic existence for all involved. Eventually, the Sisters would be sharing efforts with Reverend Jemison's church in aiding the Black community.

At a later date the Sisters would focus on meeting more imposing needs, such as health care, vocational training, and education, but the first order of business was bringing as many souls into membership in the Catholic Church. Multiple entries in correspondence and annals note the number of baptisms, or catechumens. Even after the school and the hospital were established, the numbers of conversions to the Catholic faith would continue to be noted.

This is not to say that the emphasis on conversions was a bad thing; when the Sisters organized a Sodality for the women of St. Elizabeth Parish, they provided a social setting for women and a sense of pride in membership. Sister Frances Marie, in a report to the Rochester Motherhouse dated February 22, 1941 noted: *The salvation of Selma lies in the moral uplifting of its women.*

In a subsequent letter to Mother Rose Miriam, Sister Frances Marie opined that "no lasting good will be done here unless there is a school." She felt that a school could improve especially the lot of the girls, who carried the burdens of family and of moral upbringing of the children.

The young men we meet at recreation—there we have at least trained them to stand up and say, 'good evening, Sister'. Ask a child where his father is—he is dead, don't know, or in Birmingham. Of course these conditions are accompanied by the serious social diseases. Even with [a school], it would take three generations to bring about a change. A great deal of the evil is caused from poverty plus ignorance. We are going to start a Sodality soon. (Letter from Sister Frances Marie to Mother Rose Miriam, October 8, 1940).

Special observances were conducted by the women's Sodality, and it gave them a chance to have a say in their own lives. Miss Martha Esther Jones could not have expressed it better:

Us women now have a sodality of our own and we will beat them men clean to pieces with our spirituality (Letter of Queen Esther Jones to the Sisters, February 22, 1941).

With all of the responsibilities the women shouldered, including childbearing and rearing, housework, odd jobs for extra money, and almost sole responsibility for the support of family, the participation of these women in a Church organization is testament to their grit. The recognition they received as members of this Sodality must have been heartening.

The subsequent establishment of a similar organization for the men rounded out a reason for active membership in the Catholic Church: one should be proud of his or her practice of the Faith. The public espousal of their Catholic faith exposed the Black Catholics, men and women, to ridicule and opposition of those suspicious of Roman Catholicism. Nonetheless, they proudly persisted.

The population of St. Elizabeth's parish was about 400, but this was a rather "loose" approximation because church attendance tended to be sporadic, driven by impassable roads in the rainy season, bouts of sickness among the members of the community, opportunities for employment elsewhere, and major and minor tragedies among the families. But, as was seen in subsequent events, the pride of the Black community in their church and school would be palpable

NO TIME FOR IDLING

SISTER MARY ELLEN DUNDON wrote, on September 20, 1940, the day after their arrival:

> Sisters Anastasia, and Frances Marie made their first visit to East Selma today, accompanied by Father Bouffard. They met Ella and George Davis and then they went to see Georgia Vasa who is probably suffering from venereal disease. The next house was that of Melia Murty and Lulu Branley who appeared to be respectable old ladies. After instructing the two they visited Lulu Owen, a parishioner who had built her own corn crib out of logs about 8 inches in diameter. A few other calls were made and they met Judge Washington who has been seriously ill. In the meantime, Sister Francis de Sales and myself walked down to the post office. The whole street was out to see us on the way back (Letter to Mother Rose Miriam, September, 20, 1940).

In fact, the first several weeks after the Sisters' arrival were spent visiting the people of Selma and of excursions to the more rural areas to meet with people who, in the 21st century, would have been considered "off the grid". If the Black folks who lived in the city of Selma were not well off, those in the rural South were a thousand times so, isolated, lacking basic services, including electricity and indoor plumbing, and invisible to the government agencies who were supposed to look out for them.

> The poor Negroes in their shacks have a hard time keeping warm in the winter. In one house last week where we were giving instructions to an old woman, the wind blew a real gale through the spaces in the floors and walls. We were received with real gratitude the next day when we returned to her with pieces of large cartons received from Rochester (Letter from Sister Frances Marie to Mother Rose Miriam).

This is not the picture that had been painted in a letter dated October

1, 1940 from an H.B. Cowell, Catholic School Division Manager for *The Instructor* magazine:

> *You will find Selma a very delightful city. There are beautiful homes and it is very historical. I hope that you will find someone to take you on a tour and show you where the first Capitol of Alabama was located.*

Needless to say, the Sisters did not find a lot of "delight", but Mr. Cowell did accompany his letter with a donation of "a few books to start building your library." Eventually, the Sisters would build and maintain the only free library specifically for Black people in the entire region.

The home visits were opportunities for the Sisters to assess needs, get to know the local Black populace, and cement a personal connection with people for whom years of promises never materialized. One must marvel at the intrepidity and courage of these Sisters who were truly "strangers in a strange land" but who doggedly pursued their ministry. The visits and the attempts to get to know Black parishioners and non-parishioners alike shaped the plans and strategies that the Sisters would realize in institutionalizing the efforts to ameliorate the dreadful conditions of Black people, educate them, and set them on a path of self-sufficiency.

In a memoir, Sister Francis David Backman remembered the home visits:

> *I recall just walking the streets in the Black neighborhood, speaking to those who answered us, sitting on porch steps and talking freely to brave souls who dared to talk with us, even entering their homes and sharing talk freely with them. Of course it took a while but we found many old, ill, neglected people. The children were more open and free than the adults who wondered just who and what we were in black habits but were obviously happy at white folks talking to them.*

In addition to the home visits, the Sisters were constantly entertaining visitors from the North, and those "passing through".

> *Mr. and Mrs. George Gurnow from the Motherhouse in Pittsford visited us today. They were down for their son Bill's graduation at Maxwell Field, (Archives March 8, 1941).*

Father Larkin called and spent the evening telling tales of his trip North and delivering messages from our friends there. (March 10, 1941).

The Mercy's came down for supper. (December 26, 1940)

Sister de Chantal's niece from Boston called on us. (January 27, 1941)

Father Alberic Van Hal, a Cistercian from Paulding, Mississippi, came today and stopped in for dinner.(February 4, 1941).

Father Connell of Rochester stopped at the convent today and said Mass. (November, 1949).

And so on and on. Streams of visitors, Sisters from Rochester and elsewhere, and Sisters' families stopped in on the Sisters who happily provided bed and board. It must have been a welcome relief to see familiar faces and hear familiar accents; but it must also have been difficult to see those people who might never understand the Sisters' desire to come to Alabama.

SELMA, ALABAMA

SELMA, ALABAMA WAS NAMED, in 1865, the county seat of Dallas County. It lies on the Alabama River, crossed by the now famous Edmund Pettus Bridge. The name of the city has evolved; from Ecor Bienville to Moore's Bluff to be named Selma after a poem by James Macpherson Ossian, a Scottish poet, and the city was incorporated in 1820. Selma was notable for its position on the Alabama River, and was an important port during the reign of "King Cotton" when the cotton growers needed to get their crops to Northern markets where factories turned cotton into clothing.

During the Civil War (1861-1865), Selma became important to the Confederacy because of its extensive munitions plants. But the Battle of Selma on November 2, 1865, in which the Union army routed the Confederate defenders of the city, was a terrible disaster. Not only did the Union army defeat the Southern contingent, but, consistent with the "slash and burn" policies of General William Tecumseh Sherman, the Union army leader, the city was demolished, its manufacturing plants razed, public buildings burned, and its citizens subject to Union army occupation until 1876.

During Reconstruction and the establishment of the Freedman's Bureau, Black men were elected as congressmen and city council members. Former slaves, however, only had rudimentary education, and few skills, beyond the menial, and their influence was both ephemeral and token. The Federal government provided reparations for slavery in terms of their being able to farm the land on which they had previously worked for someone else. In fact, word quickly spread that the government was giving away "forty acres and a mule." But this newly-found wealth was quickly snatched away. Andrew Johnson, a Southern white man, and successor to Abraham Lincoln upon his assassination, persuaded the former plantation owners to visit Washington to pay fealty to the Federal government, which most of them did. In return, he ceded to them the ownership of the land that had been seized after the war and mandated for the Freedman's Bureau. In the meantime, the Congressional Republicans refused to admit Southern representatives to Congress unless their states ratified the fourteenth and fifteenth amendments. Having secured citizenship and Black men's right to vote, the Federal government promptly forgot about the South and, by the end of the nineteenth century, things were pretty much back to *status quo ante bellum*. Moreover, Black people migrated north to the big cities to secure manufacturing jobs, leaving a depleted population in places like Selma. Those who stayed eventually lost the land that they had been apportioned, land which was quickly snatched up by white farmers who leased it back to those who became tenant farmers. Thus, the Black farmers were relegated, once again, to working the land for someone else.

Backlash to the newly-won civil rights was inevitable, and the Ku Klux Klan, the American Know-Nothing Party, and militia-type organizations sprang up to restore the old order. These groups did not just oppose Black people; as equal opportunity haters, they rallied against immigrants, Catholics, and any other group that did not match their ideal of who was to be in charge of the country. Because nature abhors a vacuum, these groups rushed in during the nineteenth and twentieth centuries to fill the void left by the short attention span of the Federal government.

To be fair, however, there was a goodly share of white people in Selma after the era of Reconstruction (1865-1890) who cared about the Black people of Selma. As will be seen below, at one time Selma had two hospitals that tended to Black patients, and a number of programs, including lunch programs that kept Black families fed during the depths of the Great Depression (1930-1940). The plethora of religious organizations in Selma made it a center of efforts to improve the lot of Black citizens, and, if the events of the 1965 Selma- to -Montgomery March cast a pall on the citizenry of Selma, it also uncovered the latent desire to improve access to civil rights among those citizens who were neither members of the local constabulary nor the more vocal white supremacists.

Selma prospered during the 1920s, and there were plans for great public works projects, including a "new hotel to outdo anything of its kind of any city in the state of Alabama". (Fitts, 2016, p. 192). Unfortunately, the Great Depression hit Selma especially hard. Sixty-three banks in Alabama could not weather the disaster. Even worse, Selma's two major employers, Alabama Textile Mills and Sunset Mills were both felled by the economy, and hundreds of Selmians, black and white, were without jobs. When, in 1931, the Baptist Convention sought to close the Baptist Hospital, a group of physicians leased, for ten years, the two Baptist hospitals, so that there would be health care available for both Blacks and whites. One of those hospitals would eventually be purchased by the Edmundites and staffed by the Sisters of St. Joseph.

The Selma Relief Association, in 1931, catalogued the details of their relief work in the *Selma Times Journal* of February 12, 1931:

> *During the month of January $1,177.25 was spent for relief among white families of Selma, and $1,005.21 among colored (sic) families of Selma and Dallas County. Food was issued during the month to 132 white families and work was provided for many white men who applied for food...A total of 727 negro families was cared for in city and county (Fitts, 2016, p. 193).*

Significantly, Black employees of the Selma Manufacturing Company had ten per cent of their wages garnished for relief of Black citizens (Fitts, 2016, p. 193). Thus the residents of Selma demonstrated concern for the plight of their Black neighbors.

But other areas were not so kind to the Black community. Summary justice, including lynching was imposed for any "crime" from looking at a white woman to labor organizing. Poll taxes and literacy tests kept Blacks from approaching the polls and they were barred from even serving on juries. Thus while Selmians tended to the physical needs of Black citizens, the full employment of their civil rights was sharply curtailed.

When the Great Depression hit, in 1929, it hit the South especially hard, due to the fact that agriculture was still the dominant industry in the South at that time. While the 1920s had seen a great Black migration from the South to Northern cities such as New York, Detroit, and Chicago, it was to bring a great cultural renaissance to the Black community. The huge migrations of the 1930s, however, were desperate attempts to flee the grinding poverty in the South and seek the solace and services of the cities, thus creating the great ghettos such as Harlem and the South Side of Chicago.

In addition, those fleeing the South had been farmers, and their departure further disrupted the production of food and cotton. Those who remained experienced a degree of poverty that is hard to imagine in the present day, as social, familial, and economic supports collapsed despite efforts to the contrary.

Relief programs that had looked so promising as to bring the Roosevelt New Deal to fruition in the South were thwarted by white Dixiecrats who had swiftly seized political power upon the abandonment of the North. Sister Mary Ellen Dunden wrote on October 18, 1940:

> Sister Anastasia visited Rebecca Smith and Judge Washington and learned that they didn't receive their week's allowance of food from the city officials, the same was true of Georgia Vass, another sick parishioner.

Education and health care had become an embarrassment . Here is the description of the local public school:

> I have never seen such a tumble-down shack in my life. There must have been about 150 youngsters ranging from about 5 years to 21. There were two rooms, no door between, just a rough partial wall. We saw no books or equipment. The blackboard was merely several feet of wall. The seats and desks were made of rough, long planks, nailed together (Sister Frances Marie).

Likewise, Sister Anastasia looked in on one of the "hospitals" that would serve the Blacks. She noted:

> Visited the Booker T. Washington Emergency Home run by the Baptists. The front steps are treacherously rickety, the back steps made of orange crates. No bed clothes visible in rooms which did not have a single window.

The plight of the Black children was always on the minds of the Sisters. Certainly their poverty contributed greatly to their general lack of good health; it was up to the Sisters to ferret out the causes. In one of the letters to Father Randall back in Rochester, Sister Frances Marie wrote in 1950:

> Sister noted that Johnny Allen demonstrated a lethargy that was not normal. We found out that his problem was due to malnutrition. Thanks to our friends in the North, Johnny and his family are

eating better. This may eventually solve the trouble. Could be, the
listless father is just too hungry to work.

In spite of being almost overwhelmed by the basic needs of the people whom they visited, the discovery of the importance of the Clothes Room marked an understanding of the "coin of the realm": clothing. Countless entries in the annals of the mission note the work in the clothes room. Donations of used clothing from drives in the parishes of the North were valuable commodities. Nor were these simply given away; a nominal charge was imposed, and some days the Sisters netted paltry amounts. Sister Anastasia wrote: *Today, after five hours in the Clothes Room, we ended up with $.18.* Later, when she needed help cleaning up the Colored infirmary, Sister Anastasia went downtown and enlisted jobless men with the promise of clothes for any work they could do.

The war (1941-45) brought some measure of economic help to the Selma area as Craig Air Force Base was established as a center for training pilots. and populated by airmen from all over the country. The armed forces, however, were still not integrated, and would not be so until the end of the war. Remarkably Black airmen, though billeted in separate barracks, received training at Craig (Fitts, 2016, p. 207). The presence of the base also presented the opportunity for some employment, however menial, among the Black people of Selma. The base provided an opportunity for the Sisters to do some catechizing. Eventually, through cultivated friends on the base, the Sisters were included in many social activities sponsored by Craig Air Force Base.

On February 9, 1943, Sister Frances Marie wrote to Sister Helene regarding the effect of the war effort on the Black people of Selma:

> *The colored (sic) folks are benefitting in some ways through war*
> *conditions. The large cities are offering high wages, but not being*
> *trained in the art of spending, there is a question as to how much*
> *they will save. The young men are in the army and the women have*
> *accepted positions in the North. (SSJ Archives)*

Eventually, Bush Hog, a manufacturer of agricultural equipment, and International Paper built factories in Selma, but the lack of education among the Black residents of Selma, the lack of trustworthy transportation, and *de facto* segregation prevented even private industry from being a source of economic security for Black people, and for Black folks, the prosperity wrought by World War II largely left untouched the plight of Black men and women.

To combat the nullification of equal opportunity legislation largely supported in the North, a bevy of so-called "Jim Crow" laws grew rampant in the South. In addition, the 1896 Supreme Court decision in *Plessy v. Ferguson*, which granted "separate but equal" facilities in political, educational, and daily life pretty much put the stamp of approval on separate facilities for Whites and for Blacks, which, by the 1954 case, *Brown v. Board of Education*, demonstrated that separate was not equal. Needless to say, Supreme Court decisions, for the poor Black inhabitants of Selma and its surroundings, left their plight untouched.

Even by 1978, thirteen years after the great and bloody push for civil and economic equality, a report to the Motherhouse by the Selma community reported:

> *In 1975 unemployment in Dallas County averaged 9.9%. In 1970 22.2% of all families in Selma (with 52% of the population being Black) had incomes less than $3000. (Selma Update, March 1, 1978)*

That was the year that the local air base, Craig Air Force Base, was shuttered.

> *About 7,100 persons (out of a Dallas County population of 56,000) were directly affected by the closure. The area's population could be lowered by 9.5% and unemployment could increase to 19.8% in Dallas County (Selma Update, March 1, 1978).*

Undeterred by the opposition of many in Selma, Sister Frances Marie, perhaps with some pride, reported in the summer of 1950:

> *The work being done here by the Catholic Church is at least gaining local recognition, for last February our buildings were part of a group that were marked with KKK stickers. Several Colored people, particularly the more prominent ones received notices from the same organization to get out of town.*

Unfortunately, the bishops of Southern dioceses subscribed to the application of the ruling in *Plessy*: if "separate but equal" applied to other parts of the polity, so, too, was it applicable to the Catholic Church. Thus separate Black and white parishes, schools, and hospitals bore the same cross of Christ, but for different adherents. This policy of the Bishop of Alabama was to have consequences as the Civil Rights efforts began to be felt.

Time and time again, the Sisters tried to confront the "establishment" to secure for the Black people what had been deemed rightfully theirs. Even paltry food vouchers and chits for medicine provided huge battles for those for whom they were intended.

> *We learned this week that a number of our people were not receiving their rations from the Relief Office. Two of us walked over to the center on the other side of the city and when we arrived in the alley there were about two hundred waiting, such a hungry destitute crowd you could hardly imagine. As we passed along slowly, their faces lighted up and they made sure no one would obstruct our path. Inside there were supplies enough or an army but only a few clerks slowly doing up packages. We learned that our friends had not received any food for several days, the excuse being that so much food had come in there was no time to deal it out. Not one of the two hundred received a bite to eat today. I am quite sure, however, that they will not be refused again* (September 26, 1940).

The Selma that the Sisters found in 1940 consisted of two worlds: The white population and the Black people. Jim Crow laws had erased the heady time of Reconstruction and the conferral of civil rights on the former slaves. Separate facilities, such as schools, drinking fountains, public restrooms, hospitals, and transportation-all well-documented in myriad testimonials were the order of the day. The "separate "part of segregation never lived up to the "equal" part, as Black –designated facilities were shoddier, more worn out, and of poorer quality.

The Selma of the 1960s would be a more optimistic place, with hope for true equality sitting just outside one's reach, but with that hope in sight. The confluence of protest and social program legislation would offer an opportunity for change and the promise of better days.

The question of why Selma, Alabama became the flashpoint for the civil rights protests lies in the fact that, although there were over 15,000 Black people of voting age in Selma in 1961, only 156 were registered to vote. Deterrents were many: poll taxes, "literacy" tests, and Sheriff Jim Clark 's acts of intimidation were enough to ensure that the voter rolls were devoid of Black men and women. Frustration with orderly processes to secure voting rights led to what became known as Bloody Sunday and its aftermath.

But, today, decades after the heady 1960s, Selma could also be dubbed " the town that time forgot", as, almost 60 years after its notoriety as a center for the struggle for civil rights, Selma is riddled with poverty and joblessness, and all their concomitant ills. Two hundred years after its founding, an inhabitant in 2020 summed up the situation in present-day Selma:

> *There are no jobs in Selma. Especially if you got a record, and almost everyone in Selma has a record.*

Another, working at stripping cement off of old bricks that he could sell, mused:

> *'This is slave work, that's what it is, but the only work around. Kind of funny when you think about it, because them bricks were probably made by slaves. That's Selma for you, though: still a city of slaves.' (Arnade, 2016)*

In his article of February 4, 2016, Chris Arnade, a photographer who has documented the lives of poor Americans wrote in *The Guardian*:

> *You see the ugliness of poverty that is modern Selma: dilapidated and boarded-up homes tagged with gang symbols, empty lots littered with vodka bottles and fast food wrappers, and sterile low-income projects.*

THE LIFE OF THE SISTERS

As HAS BEEN NOTED previously, the daily horarium, or schedule of the Sisters was not immediately altered to conform to the vastly different circumstances in which they found themselves. The Sisters continued to follow a Holy Rule which had been the source of guidance for Sisters of St. Joseph for 300 years, and which had been formulated for a different continent, a different time, and a different culture.

Carol Coburn and Martha Smith (1999) note that Sisters arriving in the United States from various countries during the 19th century, had a lot more freedom than Sisters of the 20th century. In 1917, the Vatican issued a *motu proprio* , or mandate that took sisters back 600 years to hew more closely to what the Church envisioned that sisters ought to be and do. Sisters were to be more subservient to bishops and clergy in general, observe a quasi-cloistered existence, do what they were told, and generally know "their place" in the Church. After the Second Vatican Council (1962-65) and the cultural revolution of the 1960s, this would have a boomerang effect that would change the landscape of religious life to an unprecedented degree.

As has been noted above, Sundays saw the Sisters attend three Masses, conduct catechism classes in the afternoon, attend Rosary and Benediction, and then supervise the youth activities in the evening. The Sisters rotated trips to Rochester for their annual retreat, and faithfully renewed their vows in the parish church every July 2, the Feast of the Visitation.

At their arrival, the Sisters were installed in a sturdy brick house on Broad Street next to the Baptist Church. They quickly made friends with the Sisters of Mercy, who operated the white Catholic school. The annals mention many visits of the Sisters of Mercy for picnics, dinners, and feast day celebrations. These visits were reciprocated by the Sisters of Mercy and provided a social outlet in a place that was most challenging and could invite sadness and despair.

In addition to the visits by the Sisters of Mercy, family members from Rochester visited occasionally, as did members of other religious congregations and visiting clergy. Bishop Toolen visited from Mobile, and Mother Rose Miriam looked in on her pet project. Besides visiting parishioners in their homes and hospitals, the Sisters provided gracious hospitality to myriad visitors.

There were several challenges to the Sisters' enculturation, beginning with the fact that they did not own a car. They were dependent on the priests for transportation and, because Selma lacked any public transportation, they walked. However, on Christmas Day, 1940, their very first Christmas in Selma, Father Randall from Rochester, gifted them with a car, and the Sisters could now control their activities more easily. Although the war brought severe gasoline shortages and concomitant rationing, Father Randall always made provision for the Sisters to have fuel for their car.

The annals are full of anecdotes about Sisters' families and friends visiting Selma. During the war, Sister Frances Marie's nephew, Bob, was stationed at Craig Air Force Base, and spent many a Sunday enjoying dinner with his aunt and the Sisters. It must have been a welcome break for both him and the Sisters. There are also several entries that describe repasts, celebrations, and special occasions with the Edmundite fathers, who reciprocated in kind. The only omission is parishioners' and local people's being able to visit with the Sisters in their house.

It is important to note that the Sisters' presence, their close work with adults and children, and their attention to the needs of the community not only endeared them to the parishioners, but blurred racial lines that might have served to divide the Sisters from the Black community.

> Little Shirley Mae, aged five years, was playing a game with one of the Sisters tonight. It consisted simply of hiding things in Sister's hands and guessing which one contained the coveted prize. She selected the wrong hand at one point and gleefully Sister held her palm out, saying 'it's empty!' Shirley was quiet for a minute. Then, taking Sister's hand in both her tiny ones, she held it up close to her face and said, ' Sister, why yo hand white?'

The subsequent development of the Selma mission, the evolution of the school and the hospital, and the concomitant agitation for civil rights for the Black people transformed the daily life of the Sisters. Sisters from other congregations came to Selma after the Bloody Sunday events of March, 1965, finding there a hub of interest in helping Black people to improve their lot. Often these efforts were dilettantish, and short-lived. In any case, the Sisters made everyone feel welcome and made constant efforts to maintain a cohesive community.

> *Even the convent life has changed. Formerly the convent housed only Sisters of St. Joseph(of Rochester). Today it is also the home of two other religious communities, Carondelet Sisters of St. Joseph and Daughters of Charity, who help staff Good Samaritan Hospital.*

> *The combined convent arrangement is a happy one. House government and duties are shared. Also shared are religious exercises of the Sisters, and recreational activities. The three communities for one convent family enjoying a special mission spirit of unity. (Annals of Selma Sisters, 1975).*

Three years later, Sisters Shirley Casler, Maureen Finn, and Mary Jane Mitchell began another community house.

The community annals for 1978-1979 contain this explanation:

> *The decision to form a separate house from the convent on Broad Street was reached during a meeting in Selma with Sister Jamesine (congregational president at that time) in August, 1978. Sisters Shirley Casler, Maureen Finn and Mary Jane Mitchell decided to form a community which would have as a goal a simple life style and response to our call to poverty. After looking for a house for several weeks, a house at 1313 St. Ann Street was found and rented on September 20, 1979. Following cleaning and painting, the sisters spent their first night in their new home on September 29, the day Pope John Paul I died. Furnishings came from yard sales, the Broad Street convent, and sister Jane Kelly (a CSJ from St. Louis) (Annals of Selma Community, 1978-1979).*

A short addendum at the end of the 1978-79 annals notes:

> *Our salary increased during the year from $3300 to $4200 to*

meet the Diocesan salary, with each sister getting $50 a month for
living needs. We shared all our money and belongings in common,
not taking a personal allowance.

It is interesting to note, also, that, in the next 25 years, 38 sisters from communities other than the Rochester Sisters of St. Joseph came to Selma to live and work with the SSJ's. With the exception of Sister Jane Kelley, CSJ (who still resides in Selma), and Sister Rosanne Cook, CSJ, most of them stayed no longer than three years, and many for only a year.

THE SCHOOL

IN 1880, THE SOCIETY of Jesus (Jesuits) arrived in Selma and took over the ministerial duties of Assumption parish, a whites-only church. Resolved to make

Selma a center of education, (Fitts, 2016, p. 133) they recruited the Madames of the Sacred Heart, who, in 1881, established a school, Sacred Heart Academy, for white girls. Within a year, they also opened St. Andrew's School for Boys, but the Madames left Selma in 1891, and the boys' school closed that same year. The Sisters of Mercy, however, took over the girls' school, and converted it into a coeducational elementary (grades 1-8) school for white children. They continued its operation until 1971, when St. Elizabeth's School, for Black children, and Assumption School for white children, merged. In that year, the Sisters of Mercy withdrew from Selma altogether.

As has been noted above, the education of the Black children in the public schools in Alabama of the 1940's was in shambles. In fact, to this day, (2020) the state of Alabama ranks 50th among the United States in educational achievement. As of this writing (2020), the public schools in the city of Selma report an average of 24% of children reading at or above grade level, and 23% at or above grade level in math (US Dept. of Education website, November 10, 2020). In 1940, any quality education of Black children was practically nonexistent.

We drove out the Montgomery Road to find Sophie Jackson's school (the Black schools were simply named after whoever was the head of school). *The building, though very tumble-down, was not as bad as one we had visited earlier, probably because, on Sunday, it served as the Bethel M.E. Church. Several children recited poems but we were unable to understand much that was said-they enunciate very poorly (January 6, 1941.)*

Several academies existed in the Selma area, even schools and academies owned and operated by Protestant churches, but these, too, were restricted to white children. There was nothing resembling a quality education for Black children. But this was precisely why the Sisters of St. Joseph had been recruited to Selma: to establish and operate a school. And so it happened.

Sisters of St. Joseph in Rochester, New York were mainly known as educators. They staffed multiple schools of the Diocese of Rochester, as well as Nazareth Hall, an elementary school for boys, Nazareth Academy and St. Agnes High Schools for girls, and several Diocesan high schools. They also owned, operated, and staffed Nazareth College for women.

To clarify, the Sisters had been teaching since the moment they arrived. They conducted catechism classes among adults and children, and note, numerous times, that their visits to the homebound and elderly included "instruction". By this means, when they did open a school, they had already secured their place as trusted educators with the Black community of St. Elizabeth's Parish.

The Sisters knew that they needed to reconnoiter the area to see what was being done in the area of Catholic education. Since securing a car, in December of 1940, the Sisters had visited, on many occasions, other Edmundite establishments, most notably, the mission on Mon Louis Island. There were three "colored" schools on the island: St. Philip's, St. Michael's, and St. Margaret's. On May 8, 1941, the Sisters drove over to Montgomery where they visited another of the Black schools, St. Jude's, and observed the classes in session. The next day, they visited the Sisters of Mercy school in Montgomery; that school was for white Catholics.

Undeterred by the fact that they did not have a dedicated school building, nor did they have materials, the Sisters opened a school with just a kindergarten. If it were successful, the upper grades, one by one, would be added until there were eight grades plus a kindergarten. And so on February 10, 1941, the first session of kindergarten was held in the front room of the parish house with six pupils in attendance. As Sister Mary Ellen Dundon explained it, "Registration is limited to the children of the parishioners and advanced catechumens to start with."

The Sisters expected the weeping and gnashing of teeth that goes with the first day of school, but found the youngsters didn't want to go home, even when school was finished! They thought they were in fairyland (February 10, 1941).

The school, conducted in crowded conditions in the parish house, which also included the social center, a religious instruction room and the ever-popular clothes room, provided more than lessons in academia. It was the instrument through which the Sisters could secure basic services for the children. They were taken to the local dental clinic, they were provided needed vaccinations, and the school was visited more than once by doctors. In addition, the Sisters were able to keep in touch with the students' families (no one had a phone) by checking on attendance and making visits to the homes of children chronically absent. In this way the Sisters could ascertain and try to meet the basic needs of the families for food, clothing, and medical help. Sister Frances Marie, in a taped interview in 1971 observed that a nutritious meal was provided to the children, half of it paid for by a government program, and the other half by the mission.

The National Lunch Program does much toward building up our children physically for many of the children come to school with little or no breakfast. The children are trained to eat nourishing foods and to eat the food served. It is surprising how much patience and watchfulness can accomplish in building up good eating habits. During the last school year (1948-49) 13,271 meals were served-the government contributing $1,197.39 and commodities. The Clothes Room contributed the balance: $965.59. (1949)

Thus the paltry sums realized by the now notable Clothes Room made a huge difference in the lives of the parishioners' children.

At the same time the Sisters were beginning St. Elizabeth's School for the education of children, they opened a library for the children and adults, since Black people were forbidden access to the so-called "public" library. Sister Francis David recalled:

I had met a few high school pupils who joined me at games in the front rooms. One evening one of them exclaimed that they had a failing mark and believed it was unfair. They had been given an assignment to do some research and write it up, but there was no library in school and Blacks were not allowed in the public library. I immediately wrote to several of our schools back home in Rochester, for any reference books they could spare. In a short time we were flooded with encyclopedias, etc. (Memoir of Sister Francis David Backman, 1994).

Sister Vincentine Broderick wrote, in spring of 1947:

Last October we opened a library for the Colored(sic) of the city and surrounding vicinity. The opening night was very dismal, for in spite of newspaper announcements and much publicizing by way of the spoken word, not a soul appeared. We persevered however and today we have a well-organized reference and reading library well patronized by many of Selma's Colored citizens.

She reported that most of the patrons of the library were children, and that the Sisters were able to direct and suggest their reading selections. But she wryly noted:

It is laughable to see the Reverends from our Baptist Theological Seminary come in to prepare their sermons from the works of Fulton Sheen. Perhaps it will be a means of spreading the Faith, too, as a woman stopped one of the Fathers on the street and asked about the doctrine of Purgatory. She said that she had accompanied her children to the library to do some work and picked up a religion book to read while waiting.

Year by year the school added a grade, and, though there was no dedicated school building, the Sisters did what they could, oftentimes preferring to ask pardon before permission. In a letter to Mother Rose Miriam, Father Casey reported:

…[Y]ou were right thinking there was not an accommodation for a second class room. The fact is, they (the Sisters) just took another room which was being used for recreation (Letter of September 27, 1941).

GROWTH AND ACCREDITATION

As the school grew, although it would never have more than 160 students, supervisors from the Diocesan education office in Mobile visited, as well as a supervisor from the state education department. The Sisters learned that they needed to be certified with the Diocese of Mobile (but not by the State of Alabama), and this could be achieved by their attendance at the Diocesan Teachers' Convention. They attended the Third Annual Meeting of the Teachers of the Diocese of Mobile on September 18 and 19, 1941 in Birmingham, AL. A letter dated July 7, 1949 from Sister Vincentine Broderick, then the local superior, to Sister Alma Joseph in Rochester, accompanied the forms required by the Diocese of Mobile to certify the teachers at St. Elizabeth School, so that they might be filled out as Sisters were assigned to the school.

Three months after the school had been started, Mother Rose Miriam, who visited Selma several times during her time in office as Superior General, wrote to the pastor of St. Vincent's Church in Churchville, NY, to acknowledge a donation to the mission:

> As a social worker who visited Alabama recently expressed it, our Sisters are trying to combine all the best of the modern with the zeal of the first Christians in caring for the Negroes. Their little school compares favorably with the best in the Rochester Diocese. (December 11, 1941)

Rumors of expanding the school in order to expedite an end to segregation in the school flew about in 1950. Sister Vincentine wrote to Mother Rose Miriam what were to be prophetic words:

> Wild rumors! The [Edmundite] Fathers are taking over the white parish and are building a school for both whites and blacks— no segregation!! Can you imagine any rumor more ridiculous? The Fathers have more than they can do right now to take care of their own color without taking over the whites too!

One can imagine the ludicrous nature of such a rumor in 1950, given the implacable existence of segregation. But one wonders about the deep-seated assuredness of the continued existence of the *status quo* among these Sisters. After all, their focus was to initiate and operate *separate* education and health care for Black people, and it is not apparent in the archives nor in the correspondence that the Sisters had any desire to eradicate the systemic racism that pervaded the South.

In a letter to Mother Helene, in 1957, Sister Francis David, the Selma superior and by now the principal of St. Elizabeth's School wrote:

Thank God we do not have to worry about integration but the spirit of the movement has touched some of our children and peo-ple. Arrogance and a certain boldness which were unknown to them be for have made their appearance (Letter to Mother Helene, September 15, 1957).

To be fair, these were women of their time, and racism and even sexism were not battles to be fought, at least for the next two decades. In fact, it would seem that the chief enemy was anti-Catholicism and the chief point of pride, as seen in annual reports to the SSJ Motherhouse, and Father Randall in Rochester was the number of converts in the Black community that were received into the Church.

In a 1965 survey of 200 religious sisters who taught in Catholic schools in the South, it was discovered that not one of them taught in an integrated school. Yet, in anonymous questionnaires, every one of them said that they wanted integration but could do nothing to change the status quo. (Traxler, June, 1965).

As will be noted later, the Catholic Church of the 1940s and 1950s, that is, the bishops, in the Southern United States had no intention of upending the *status quo*; indeed, bishops of the South rarely ventured into the topic of integration. Theirs was a mindset that the biggest enemy was anti-Ca-tholicism. Speaking out on racism might put the Church in the crosshairs of the Ku Klux Klan, the American Know-Nothing party, and the so-called "Dixiecrats"- all white supremacist groups and virulently anti-immigrant, who saw the Catholic Church as a foreign entity that paid homage to a foreign potentate. Maintaining silence on this very sensitive and volatile topic at least allowed the Catholic Church to operate ministries that served the Black population.

It is obvious that the parents trusted the Sisters to educate and to care for their children. As parents' trust grew, so did enrollment grow steadily; the annals for February 24, 1951 note:

Last year's opening day saw more children than the building could hold seeking entrance, so the Parish Hall had to be surren-

dered in favor of classroom space. What September of 1951 will bring remains in the uncertain future. We pray it will bring us a new school building.

Although parents felt that school was necessary and important, for many of them it was difficult or impossible to send their children to school. In rural areas and even in small cities such as Selma, children were needed to work in order to support the farm or sharecropper contribution, or to watch younger children or infants or elderly grandparents. If the family ran a cottage industry, children were needed to make deliveries, stock shelves, babysit for the little ones, or just mind the store.

In inclement weather, especially during the rainy season, lacking any kind of busing, children had no way of traversing flooded roads or the persistent red clay mud. Furthermore, if children had shoes, these rare and precious commodities could not be risked in wet and muddy conditions. In several entries, the Sisters note that children had no rain gear, and used paper bags as umbrellas.

Finally, lack of proper nutrition, an absence of dental care, and persistent toxic and downright dangerous environments in the poor homes made children's health especially at risk. Hazardous conditions in the homes contributed to serious injuries:

...a familiar but lamentable sight greeted our eyes. Bessie Allen, age three, had been burned at home and came to the hospital to join the ranks of those poor, deformed, sad-eyed children, who spend months with us in their fight for life (June 1, 1950).

St. Elizabeth's School graduated its first eighth grade class, consisting of ten students, on June 5,1949. Surprisingly, five of them planned to attend high school., a remarkable feat, since most Black children ended their education at eighth grade. At that time the school had 86 pupils, utilizing four classrooms and four teachers. The classrooms for the older children were very crowded and new registrants had to be turned away. However, that same month Bishop Toolen ordered that every Catholic child be enrolled in a Catholic school. That not only boosted the number of children wishing to be Baptized, but it bolstered the enrollment of St. Elizabeth School by about 20. (Sister Vincentine, 1949)

As St. Elizabeth School had its first graduation in 1949, Father Rivard wrote to Mother Rose Miriam:

As you no doubt know we are going to have our first graduation from St. Elizabeth School in few weeks and we plan to hold the exercises on the first Sunday of June.

It would be nice, Reverend Mother, if you could be present for this occasion. This is a history- making event in the educational life of Selma, in which your Sisters have contributed so much. Please come, if possible. (Letter to Mother Rose Miriam, May 5, 1949).

By the time the school had all eight grades, the Sisters each taught two grades at a time; there were never more than four Sisters in the school, and even the principal taught (interview with Sister Lorraine Julien, November 25, 2020). During the summer, the Sisters conducted a vacation school so that the children would not lose the momentum they had gained during the school year, but also to provide a nutritious noontime meal daily, and to keep up with their families' needs. Teaching Sisters from Rochester volunteered their summer months and traveled to Selma to provide a quality vacation school. Most importantly, their recollections, shared with other Sisters, inspired many Sisters to volunteer for the Selma mission.

Those days in which the Sisters were expanding the school and meeting a plethora of other needs were heady indeed. In a letter to Father Randall in February of 1951, Sister Frances Marie reported on the aspirations of the Edmundite Fathers wherein she noted wryly: *"even the most audacious would hesitate to call* [them] *plans. (February 24, 1951).* These included three churches, two rectories, three new schools and the enlargement, in due time, of two others. One cannot be surprised at the Edmundites' desire to expand the mission. Witnessing the success of the school, the increased number of parishioners and those wishing to be baptized only heartened their own spirit of the mission.

A New School for the Black Children of St. Elizabeth's

With the application of excellent pedagogy for which the Sisters were noted, the school eventually outgrew its original home, the parish mission house. In February, 1952, the Edumundite priests concluded the purchase of property on Church Street, a mere two blocks from the convent, and secured an architect to design a building that would include only four classrooms to begin with, and add on as the need showed itself. Of note is the fact that the building was never expanded, but a large building behind the school eventually opened as a kindergarten. On June 18, 1952 ground was broken for the new building. Sister Vincentine, Superior for the Sisters and school principal, wrote of the event:

> Father Lambert and Sister Vincentine used the shovels. I was so green at digging that Father Lambert had to tell me to put my foot on the spade. We have waited so long for the school that it seems an unreality.

By August, Sister Vincentine provided a detailed account of the progress of the new building, and lamented the steel strike as accounting for a delay in the construction. But the excitement of the parents of children from Queen of Peace Parish and the Sisters must have been palpable. Here was a new edifice dedicated to the education of children for whom government schools cared little, and who could see a way out of their crushing poverty with the golden key to opportunity: a Catholic education.

In 1961, the school served as a haven for the Black people of Selma when the Alabama River overflowed its banks and flooded Selma. In a prelude to the role that the hospital that would occur four years later, Sister Francis David described the event in a letter to Mother Helene:

> This is the worst flood since 1919 in Selma and the only real flood most of us have ever seen. Yesterday we started getting the halls ready and by nightfall there were 45 in the library, 10 in the hallway of the school, and 57 in the hall behind the school. The number of people to be housed tonight is 236.
>
> We taught school as usual, [and] most of our flood victims are back in school but this afternoon there was constant trekking back and forth in the halls. (Letter to Mother Helene, February 28, 1961)

Sister Barbara Lum was a nurse at Good Samaritan Hospital at that time. She recalls:

> We served meals in the parish meeting place. All received tetanus booster shots from Sister Margaret Isabelle and me after sup-

per. At evening prayer, Sister Francis Mary Rossi fainted gracefully from her kneeler, and the sisters caught her. (Interview with Sister Barbara Lum, December 26, 2020).

Though noted above, it is important to reiterate that St. Elizabeth's was not the only Catholic school in Selma. The Sisters of Mercy opened Assumption School in 1891 and had provided Catholic education to white Catholics prior to the arrival of the Sisters from Rochester. On August 4, 1952, this school underwent a change, too:

Father Lonergan of the white church has bought a large Southern mansion off the Summerfield Road for his parish school (Assumption). The Sisters of Mercy are to live in a small white house near the school. (Archives for August 4, 1952)

The new St. Elizabeth school, "modern in every detail" was built and dedicated on April 12, 1953. Bishop Toolen, who had originally invited the Sisters to Selma, gave the dedicatory talk; he praised the work of the Edmundite Fathers and gave kudos to the Sisters of St. Joseph.

A report for the 1957-58 school year listed 129 students enrolled and also noted that Catholics made up 49% of the school population. At some point, the Sisters had decided that students need not be Catholic to attend. Each of the Sisters taught two grades in one classroom. Even the principal taught a double grade, usually, grades seven and eight. Enrollment for the school was never very large, and total enrollment topped out at 160 in 1968. However, in that year, Sister Innocentia (Dolores Bachman) had 35 first and second grade youngsters in a tiny classroom. The Sister who was principal was also the superior at the convent. The Sisters also traveled annually to attend the teachers' convocations in Birmingham.

The Diocese of Mobile regularly sent supervisors to visit the school to ascertain its quality. Sister Vincentine, on November 12, 1951 describes one such visit:

Sister Alice Marie, the new Benedictine Supervisor, surprised us with her visit this morning. Luckily, work had been planned. Sisters went over to school early to get things in readiness for the day. She (Sister Alice Marie) likes the colored (sic) children and seemed to have broad sympathy. (Archives, Alabama Collection)

Sister Joan Marshall arrived in 1966 to teach fifth and sixth grades. She recalls:

> We had very small grades, even though they were double grades. I usually taught between twelve and eighteen students. Oh, they worked so hard and they were such nice kids. They had no resources at home for homework, so we had to do everything during the school day (Interview with Sister Joan Marshall, November 25, 2020).

Sister Innocentia (Dolores Bachman) taught in the school from 1968 to 1973. "When Mother Agnes Cecilia asked me to go to Selma, I had no idea what was going on." She taught grades one and two. Directives came from the Motherhouse in Rochester in 1969 that the Sisters could go back to their Baptismal names. As she tells it:

> We started school and I explained to the children that, last year they had called me Sister Innocentia, but this year they would call me Sister Dolores. From the back of the room, a student asked: 'What are we going to call you next year?' (Interview with Sister Dolores Bachman, March 3, 2021)

Selma resident John Solomon, who eventually became the assistant administrator at Good Samaritan Hospital, shared this memory:

> I didn't attend the school because I wasn't Catholic at that time, but I would see the boys from St. Elizabeth's playing basketball on the playground, and I would come over from my house to play with them. In third grade, though I still wasn't Catholic, they said I could be an altar boy and serve Mass. That was the best thing, because Sister Mary Paul, principal of the school, made sure we had something to eat after Mass. (Interview with John Solomon, February 14, 2021).

Integrating the School

The 1960s upended the stasis that the school had achieved, and demanded change that would be especially stressful for the St. Elizabeth School community. The struggle for civil rights, though protracted and painful, produced unintended consequences. When the schools of Selma were forcefully desegregated, Black children flocked to the erstwhile formerly whites-only schools, and that meant that the enrollment at St. Elizabeth's School took a hit. In her report to the Congregation, Sister Davida (Sister Joan Marshall), principal of St. Elizabeth's School, reported an enrollment of 135 pupils (July, 1969). At that time, the school's population was 50% Catholic. Even though the school had added a pre-school and a kindergarten in 1963, this was not enough to sustain the school financially.

Gradually, as the civil rights movement, and legislation, specifically the Civil Rights Law of 1964 and the Elementary and Secondary Education Act (1965) were felt in the South, school integration became a focal point. In 1964, 2.3% of Black children had secured a place in a formerly all-white school, but by 1967 that figure was 13.9%. By the 1972-73 school year, 41% of Black children had successfully entered the former white schools (*20 Years after Brown, 1974, US Department of Education)* This was to have a have a profound effect on St. Elizabeth School.

Sister Davida (Joan Marshall) recalls the day that everything changed:

> *I recall that I was invited to a meeting at the Assumption recto-*
> *ry, and I think that the principal of Assumption (a Sister of Mercy)*
> *was there as well. Bishop May (who had succeeded Bishop Toolen*
> *in 1969) wanted to make Selma an example of the new integra-*
> *tion. I told them that a consolidation would not work, and that the*
> *white people wouldn't send their children. I just had a feeling that*
> *consolidation wouldn't work (Interview with Sister Joan Marshall,*
> *November 25, 2020).*

Integration of the schools came as the result of Bishop Toolen's order. Hite(2002) claims that Toolen had issued that order in 1964 probably as a result of the criticism he had received due to his stand in opposition to the participation of priests and nuns in the civil rights movement.

In the 1964 order ending the practice of segregation in Catholic schools, Bishop Toolen wrote, "After much prayer, consultation and advice, we have decided to integrate all the schools of the diocese. I know this will not meet with the approval of many of our people, but in justice and charity, this must be done. " (Wikipedia.org) Notably, this order was given one year before the famous March on Selma.

The consolidation utilized the two buildings: the four lower grades would be held at Assumption and the four upper grades were at St. Elizabeth. Modern upgrades such as departmentalization were added to retain the students currently enrolled. Tuition was set at six dollars per month. The Edmundites, in an effort to integrate the churches, also closed the church building at St. Elizabeth's forcing the Black people to attend Assumption, and re-named the integrated parish Queen of Peace. In an article printed by the parish in 2015 to mark the fiftieth anniversary of "Bloody Sunday", it was observed: "Those who opposed integration sometimes referred to the parishes neither as Queen of Peace nor Prince of Peace but as 'Price of Peace.'"

Due to the lack of transportation, the Black children living near St. Elizabeth's School could not reach Assumption School. Likewise, Assumption Church proved to be too far for Black Catholics from St. Elizabeth parish to attend.

Mrs. Tommie Byrd was a substitute teacher in both buildings and her children attended the school. She recalls:

> I loved working with the Sisters; they were so nice. My children especially enjoyed Sister Margarethe (Margaret Kunder); she seemed to be having more fun than the children, but they loved her. But when St. Elizabeth's School building closed it was so hard for the Black children. They had been able to walk to school and now they had to go all the way up to Summerfield Road, and that was hard. Parents had to drive them, and so many parents didn't have cars or couldn't drive their children. I was lucky; when the school was moved to Queen of Peace, my children were in high school. (Interview with Tommie Byrd, February 12, 2021).

Although the Black families were excited about sending their children to the white school, white families did not share that enthusiasm.

Sister Innocentia (Dolores Bachman), who had arrived in 1968, soon was caught up in the integration of the schools, and noted, "Really the only white families who stuck with us were not from Selma; they were from Craig Air Force Base." (Interview with Sister Dolores Bachman, March 3, 2021).

Sister Josette Capozzi, who was the last principal of St. Elizabeth's School, observed.

> The children had no problem mingling, Black and white; it was the adults who were the problem. Even at parent meetings, they counted the number of Black parents and the number of white parents in attendance, to make sure that they had sufficient representation. (Interview with Sister Josette, December 20, 2020)

Sister Lorraine Julien recalls:

> I think there were only two white families that kept their kids in the school. They tried so hard to support the integration effort, but the rest of the white parents really didn't want the integrated school. (Interview with Sister Lorraine Julien, November 26, 2020).

Moreover, while Black parents were enthused about integration, that enthusiasm swung more to the integrated public schools, which charged no tuition. Sister Davida (Joan Marshall) described the efforts by the Black parents to maintain their support for the school:

> A good number of our children from St. Elizabeth's, but not all of them, enrolled in the lower grades at the former white school. They really did try to support that school, but couldn't. There were so many problems with transportation, because, at St. Elizabeth's they could walk to school. The Edmundites did secure a bus to pick up kids for school, but that didn't really help. The kids and their parents thought a lot of the Sisters, and when we asked them to support this endeavor, they really tried. In the beginning, students from St. Elizabeth were excited, but transportation problems made it impossible.

In a radio address given on March 6, 1971 on WSAY in Rochester, NY, Bishop Joseph Hogan remarked:

> What an anomaly to have to report that, as of this past week, the vast majority [of Christians in Selma] have not yet learned Christ's message of the oneness of the human family…most recently they have resisted their bishop's efforts to integrate their schools and have resented the efforts of missionaries to help the disadvantaged black population.

The resistance of which Bishop Hogan spoke, was evident in the changes wrought at the newly-constituted Queen of Peace Catholic School. Sister Joan Marshall, principal of St. Elizabeth's during the attempted consolidation, recalled that only one white family, from Craig Air Force Base, kept their children in the school's upper grades, housed at the St. Elizabeth building. One year after the consolidation in which two buildings were to be utilized, that accommodation fell apart. With the exception of one Sister, the Sisters of Mercy left the school, and only one building remained. Sister Joan recalls:

> That summer (1971), we had to pack up everything in the St. Elizabeth School building and move to the former Assumption School building which was then called Queen of Peace. Because a kindergarten was operated in a building behind the St. Elizabeth School, it could not be moved and so the Black families even lost a kindergarten.(Interview of November 25, 2020)

CLOSING THE SCHOOL

That arrangement had lasted one year. In June, 1971, a newsletter notice from the Sisters of St. Joseph Leadership Team noted:

> The "Selma Catholic School" (integrated last year, with four upper grades at St. Elizabeth's and four lower grades at Assumption) will next year be housed in the building formerly known as Assumption School, with our Sisters and the Mercy Sisters both teaching there. This decision was made and announced by Bishop John L. May of Mobile, this past month.

The loss of the St. Elizabeth School building was profound. Sister Lorraine Julian, a teacher in the school at the time, recalls:

> The Black students suffered such a loss when their school building closed. They loved that school and it was theirs. Parents tried to be supportive, but it was so hard. (Interview with Sister Lorraine Julien, November 25, 2020)

In a last-ditch effort to boost enrollment, the Catholic newspaper, *The Catholic Week,* in September, 1975 did a feature piece on Queen of Peace School:

The school, which has an enrollment of 90 this year, is present-
ly staffed by three Sisters of St. Joseph, two lay teachers, a teach-
er's aide and a physical education instructor. An integral part of
Queen of Peace is a very supportive school board and a hard-work-
ing, productive PTA. The philosophy of Queen of Peace School is to
provide complete educational opportunities for the child to grow
as a unique person in relationship to God and others. (Know Your
Fine Diocesan Schools, The Catholic Week, September 26, 1975)

Sister Doretta Rhodes wrote a summary of her experience at Queen of
Peace School in 1980. She had taught at the school from 1970 to 1973, and
fondly remembered:

When I think of my Selma days I think of PEOPLE (sic) and
lasting friendships…I think of the school children who never saw
the difference in color.

The existence of two buildings had made it impossible to utilize any
economies of scale. For example, the St. Elizabeth building during that
one school year, 1970-1971, contained 43 students for grades 5-8. The Assumption building's enrollment was similar. So, while the motivation was
valorous, the reality in enrollment numbers was onerous. There was no
way for the school to be viable financially or even academically , given the
numbers.

To counter these efforts at integration, several private "Christian" schools
sprang up, and white parents enrolled their children in these facilities.

Sister Joan left the school and returned to Rochester at the end of the
1971 school year, but she returned for the 1974-75 school year to the con-
solidated school building at Queen of Peace and remained for just that one
year. For the 1975-76 school year, Sister Josette Capozzi was the principal of Queen of Peace School and the Religious Sisters of Mercy, as noted
above, had withdrawn from the school.

In a March, 1976 report of a Selma visit by Sister Barbara Fox, who was
very involved in inner-city education in Rochester, was sent by the Central
Administration of the Sisters of St. Joseph to conduct an assessment of the
mission. At the end of her visit, she commented:

At first glance, it is obvious that the (Queen of Peace) school is
in serious difficulty. Enrollment has steadily declined (presently 86

students), *financial difficulties are mounting, and the faculty (sis-*
ter and lay) is and has been very unstable. These are signs which
can't be ignored; it is possible that within a short time we may be
forced to withdraw from the school ministry in Selma. (March 21,
1976)

Upon further consideration, however, she offered a caveat:

After my visit, however, I would concur with your (SSJ Adminis-
trative Team) decision that withdrawal is now untimely. One final,
intensive effort should be made to stabilize the school. I think [this
task] should be attempted only if there are at least three [Sister]
volunteers. (March 21, 1976).

The school closed two months later.

Later on in her report, she lists the names of six Sisters who were approached with the idea of moving to Selma to teach in the school, but
that all had demurred. It is important to note that the original Sisters had
been assigned to Selma; that is, under their vow of obedience, they would,
without consultation, be sent to Selma. But by 1976, religious renewal had
concluded that Sisters being asked to fill an assignment be consulted and
have the ability to turn it down. Consequently, the Sisters in Selma, in 1976
submitted an insert in the Congregational newsletter:

We feel a great need for a continuing presence of Sisters in the
Selma area and in Queen of Peace Parish...we hope the list of
needs given in the "newsletter" two weeks ago didn't frighten off
anyone. The description of what areas of ministry are needed was
not meant for any one Sister. The Sisters who would come to work
in Selma would have the full cooperation of the pastor, other sis-
ters, and the laypeople, who are vitally concerned that a really good
religious education program be established. ...we believe that the
Spirit will direct our efforts and lead some Sister(s) to Selma.

Although a real effort was made to secure Sisters for the Selma mission,
no additional Sisters would come to the rescue. However, given the state of
finances, the lack of enrollment, and the difficulty that so many of the children had in being transported to Queen of Peace School, in all likelihood,
the addition of Sisters would not have sufficed to save the school.

It is important to note, too, that trends in the North were leading to Sisters' leaving schools to minister in other fields. In 1965, 97% of persons who staffed Catholic schools were Sisters, Brothers, or Priests. By 1980, only 6% of Catholic school staffs were made up of religious men and women (NCEA, 2000). Sisters were now more invested in ministering in fields of religious education, parish visiting, drug counseling, public health, and civil rights, among others.

In 1976, five weeks after Sister Barbara Fox's assessment, when the announcement that Queen of Peace School was closing was published in the Selma *Times-Journal* (April 27, 1976), the next year's enrollment would have been fewer than 50. The reporter described the school:

> *Queen of Peace School is a combination of the former St. Elizabeth and Assumption schools, opening in 1971. Open to everyone, the school had a nominal tuition fee and quality education was stressed.*

Quoting pastor Father Eymard Galligan, the article continued:

> *For a Catholic parish school to be viable, it must receive support from its parishioners... Since its beginning five years ago, our Catholic parishioners, in a steady yearly decline, have failed to send their children, for whatever reason...[T]oday, only 30 children out of over 100 eligible students attend.*

Needless to say, Father Galligan's remarks did not include the real reason for the school's demise. His "for whatever reason" certainly could have been translated: "white parents did not want their children to attend school with Black students" or: "the pain and loss to our Black community was insurmountable."

The Sisters of St. Joseph in Selma in the spring of 1976 sent a report to the congregation:

> *It is difficult, as so many of you know, to close a parish school. Here in Selma it means facing the failure of the attempt to combine two segregated parish schools, and trying to see where we go from here.*

With the consolidation of the parishes and the school in the offing, Bishop May, who had succeeded Bishop Toolen in 1969, had appointed Father

Nelson Ziter, SSE, the former pastor of St. Elizabeth's to head the merger process. After a year of maintaining two parishes, the closing of the Black parish was especially traumatic. John Crear, president of St. Elizabeth's parish council in 1971 wrote:

> I love Father Ziter. He's the man who brought me into the Church. But when Father Ziter closed our old chapel and school, and told us blacks to start coming to the white church and sending our kids to the while school, it was almost more than I could take. (Fitts, August, 1985).

If Black people found this merger painful, as they suffered the closure of their own church and school, white Catholics expressed their own pain. Mrs. Beth Robitaille, a member of the Assumption parish council recalled:

> It was quite a shock to lose the Sisters of Mercy who had taught our kids for 80 years. And I must confess I had some doubts about entrusting my first-grader to priests and nuns who had been so closely identified with civil rights. But I did it. (Fitts,, August 1985)

By June, 1976, there was neither a Catholic school, white or black, nor a Black Catholic parish in Selma.

Again, John Crear, who eventually became the administrator of Good Samaritan Hospital, reminisced:

> Selma used to have two Catholic schools and now we have none. It took a lot of faith for me to see any good coming out of all our struggle and sacrifice. (Fitts, August, 1985)

The demise of the Catholic school pushed the Sisters and the Edmundite Fathers to assess the quality and even existence of a viable religious education program. It is important to note that catechizing had begun with adults on Day One in 1940, but the religious education of children had not been formalized, although the Sisters did do some catechizing of high school students early on. While the vacation schools had included catechizing of the youngsters, there was a vacuum during the school year, and the national Catholic movement towards the provision for quality religious instruction for children in public schools was felt strongly in the South. Concomitantly, in the Black Catholic community, there existed no formal programs for the preparation of youngsters and adults for the reception of the sacraments.

Moreover, with the Sisters' inability to conduct a school, they were able, like their counterparts in the North, to embark on the conduct of other duties. By 1975, Sister Maureen Finn had been engaged to become the first parish assistant. Besides conducting the religious education program, she continued the practice of home and hospital visits and some clerical and administrative tasks.

The more rural areas, hitherto largely ignored because of the focus on the school in Selma, could now be attended to, and outreach programs could provide to residents of these pockets of poverty the services formerly restricted to the urban area of Selma.

While these were positive developments, however, the gradual "white flight" from the City of Selma to the remote suburbs, and the ensuing decline in the quality of education in the Selma public schools resulted in a *de facto* segregation that exists to this day. Moreover, in statistics stated above, the literacy and math competency rates in Selma remain woefully low, even over a half- century after the fight for civil rights.

While the school existed for twenty-five years, its effects on those who attended and who were taught by the Sisters cannot be overestimated. Richard Vassar, a pupil of Sister Francis David's memorialized the profound difference she made in his life. He was ten years old and a cripple, but Sister Francis David took him in. As Police Communications Officer for the Alabama State Troopers, he wrote:

> *This is Richard Vasser, one of your most grateful students, to you (sic) from trying to make something out of me. So vividly, I can remember your carrying me from the taxi to my classroom and bearing with my mischief all day long. Rest assured, I am deeply grateful to you, and all of my dear Sisters of St. Joseph. (Sent 1976, Sisters of St. Joseph Archives).*

Another former student, Lorenzo Todd, wrote to Sister Francis David in March, 1998:

> *I have been meaning to write you for years. I'll never forget how important St. Elizabeth's was to the Black Catholics when I was growing up. I have done a poor job of showing gratitude but you were always my favorite nun and I attribute much of my success to the foundation that you instilled in my early life.*

In a 2008 article for National Black History Month for the Archdiocese of Cincinnati, Joyce Coleman, a 1954 graduate of St. Elizabeth's School, wrote:

> *From the time I was a small child I was taught that I am loved with an everlasting love. As a matter of fact, I was brainwashed with love in [St. Elizabeth's} Catholic school. The Sisters of Saint Joseph taught me that nobody is better than I am. God sees all of us and loves us all. (Reported in Blessings, a publication of the Sisters of St. Joseph, Spring, 2021 by Monica Weiss, SSJ).*

If, in 1940, the Sisters had been missioned to reap a "magnificent harvest", it was most evident in the years to follow, years in which hundreds of Selma's Black children, after being imbued with an excellent academic preparation, as well as a moral grounding wrapped in genuine care, were able to realize their greatest potential. It has been said that the biggest task of Catholic schools is to build memories, impressions that leave a lasting mark on individuals. St. Elizabeth's School left an indelible mark on so many children. Its demise was sad, but its graduates were empowered to pass on to their children the sense of worth and wonder that the Sisters provided daily in the school.

St. Elizabeth's Church, Selma, in 1967
Photograph by Baker Hendershot
Society of Saint Edmund Archives, Saint Michael's College, Colchester, VT

St. Elizabeth's Convent, home of the Sisters of St. Joseph in Selma
Society of Saint Edmund Archives, Saint Michael's College, Colchester, VT

The first Good Samaritan Hospital
Society of Saint Edmund Archives, Saint Michael's College, Colchester, VT

St. Elizabeth's School building, opened in 1953
Society of Saint Edmund Archives, Saint Michael's College, Colchester, VT

Rev. Francis M. Casey, SSE
Society of Saint Edmund Archives, Saint Michael's College, Colchester, VT

Mother Rose Miriam Smyth
Archives of the Sisters of St. Joseph of Rochester, NY

Mother Rose Miriam Smyth on her visit to the Selma mission in 1940
Archives of the Sisters of St. Joseph of Rochester, NY

Sr. Vincentine Broderick visiting a family at their home, late 1940s
Archives of the Sisters of St. Joseph of Rochester, NY

Sr. Mary Ellen Dundon and Sr. Frances Marie Kehoe with the "junior
division" of St. Elizabeth's School, 1940-1941
Archives of the Sisters of St. Joseph of Rochester, NY

Sr. Francis David Backman (foreground) and Sr. Vincentine Broderick with students of St. Elizabeth's School, 1940s
Archives of the Sisters of St. Joseph of Rochester, NY

Classroom

Sisters with car 1940

Sisters of St. Elizabeth's Convent, ca. 1940-1941: Sr. Catherine Charlotte Hyland, Sr. Frances Marie Kehoe, Sr. Mary Ellen Dundon, Sr. Anastasia Mc-Cormick, Sr. Francis David Backman
Archives of the Sisters of St. Joseph of Rochester, NY

Visitors from the north: Sr. Alberta Hettel's sisters at St. Elizabeth's Convent with Srs. Vincentine Broderick, Francis David Backman, and Rose Adelaide Frisk, ca. 1945
Archives of the Sisters of St. Joseph of Rochester, NY

Sr. Francis Mary Rossi on a home visit, 1958
Archives of the Sisters of St. Joseph of Rochester, NY

Groundbreaking for St. Elizabeth's School, Sept. 1952
Society of Saint Edmund Archives, Saint Michael's College, Colchester, VT

Sr. Francis David Backman with eighth grade students at St. Elizabeth's School,
ca. 1959-1960
Society of Saint Edmund Archives, Saint Michael's College, Colchester, VT

Students arrive at St. Elizabeth's School, 1966
Society of Saint Edmund Archives, Saint Michael's College, Colchester, VT

Recess at St. Elizabeth's School, 1948
Archives of the Sisters of St. Joseph of Rochester, NY

Sisters visiting Craig Air Force base, early 1960s
Archives of the Sisters of St. Joseph of Rochester, NY

Community Room at St. Elizabeth's Convent, 1950s
Society of Saint Edmund Archives, Saint Michael's College, Colchester, VT

Sr. Louis Bertrand Dixon, Administrator of Good
Samaritan Hospital (1945-1964)
Archives of the Sisters of St. Joseph of Rochester, NY

Sr. Louis Bertrand Dix-
on at Good Samaritan
Hospital, 1950s
*Society of Saint Ed-
mund Archives, Saint
Michael's College,
Colchester, VT*

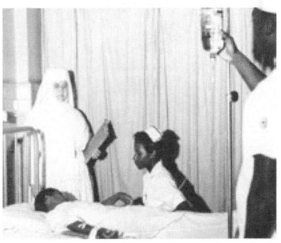

Dr. Isabel Du-
mont immunizes
Billy King, a pupil
at St. Elizabeth's
School, ca. 1950s
*Society of Saint
Edmund Archives,
Saint Michael's
College, Colches-
ter, VT*

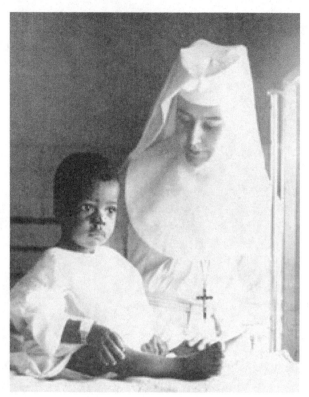

Sr. Eleanor (Barbara) Lum with a child in the pediatric ward of Good
Samaritan Hospital, 1963
Society of Saint Edmund Archives, Saint Michael's College, Colchester, VT

Mother Rose Miriam with a patient in the pediatric ward of Good Samaritan
Hospital, 1960s
Society of Saint Edmund Archives, Saint Michael's College, Colchester, VT

Sr. Margaret Isabelle Tracy with a patient in the pediatric ward of Good
Samaritan Hospital, 1960s
Society of Saint Edmund Archives, Saint Michael's College, Colchester, VT

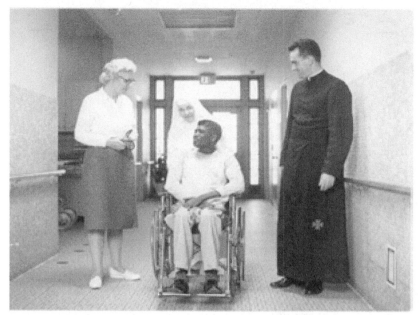

Dr Isabel Dumont, Sr. Mary Roch Basso, and Fr. Maurice Ouellet with
Thomas Mason, a resident of Good Samaritan Nursing Home, 1963
Society of Saint Edmund Archives, Saint Michael's College, Colchester, VT

Sr. Louis Bertrand Dixon instructing the first students at Good Samaritan
Hospital School of Nursing, 1950
Society of Saint Edmund Archives, Saint Michael's College, Colchester, VT

Members of the first graduating class,
Good Samaritan Hospital School of Nursing, 1950
Society of Saint Edmund Archives, Saint Michael's College, Colchester, VT

Sr. Liguori Dunlea with students at
Good Samaritan Hospital School of Nursing, 1960s
Society of Saint Edmund Archives, Saint Michael's College, Colchester, VT

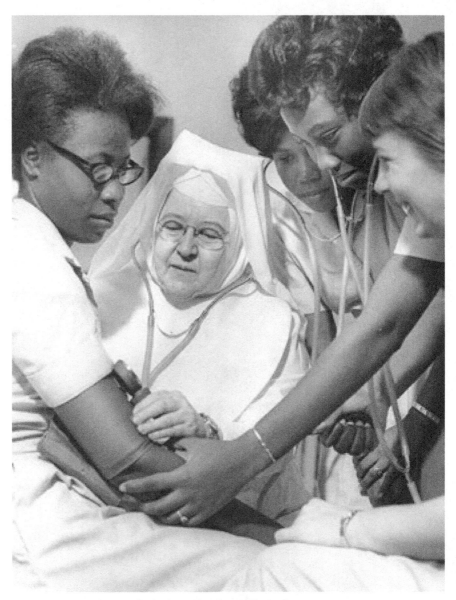

Sr. Liguori Dunlea with students at
Good Samaritan Hospital School of Nursing, 1960s
Society of Saint Edmund Archives, Saint Michael's College, Colchester, VT

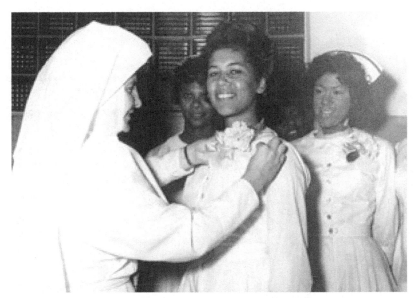

Sr. Mary Christopher Kuchman with graduates of
Good Samaritan Hospital School of Nursing, 1960s
Archives of the Sisters of St. Joseph of Rochester, NY

Rev. Norman Lambert, SSE,
Director of the Edmundite Southern
Missions, 1948
*Society of Saint Edmund Archives,
Saint Michael's College, Colchester, VT*

Fathers of St. Edmund at the
Southern Missions, 1940s
*Society of Saint Edmund Archives,
Saint Michael's College, Colchester,
VT*

One of the Edmundite Fathers making house calls in Selma, ca. 1960
Society of Saint Edmund Archives, Saint Michael's College, Colchester, VT

Rev. John Crowley, SSE, and the Sisters of
St. Joseph in the Selma mission, 1965
Society of Saint Edmund Archives, Saint Michael's College, Colchester, VT

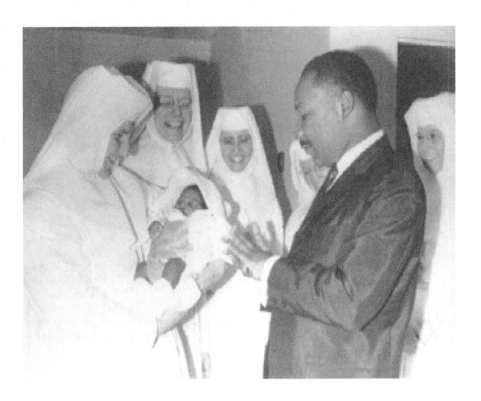

Left to right: Sisters Josepha Twomey (holding baby Synethia Perkins), Bernice (Dorothy) Quinn, Felicitas (Mary) Weaver, Margaret Isabelle Tracy, and Mary Paul Geck greet Dr. Martin Luther King, Jr., at Good Samaritan Hospital, 1965
Society of Saint Edmund Archives, Saint Michael's College, Colchester, VT

Ernest and Emma Twomey, parents of Sr. Josepha, visiting the Sisters of St. Joseph at St. Elizabeth's Convent, 1964
Archives of the Sisters of St. Joseph of Rochester, NY

Clergy and women religious who came to Selma to support the voting rights marches after Bloody Sunday were provided with simple accommodations at Good Samaritan Hospital.
Society of Saint Edmund Archives, Saint Michael's College, Colchester, VT

Sisters of other Congregations who came to Selma to support the voting rights marches after Bloody Sunday enjoy a meal at Good Samaritan Hospital provided by the Sisters of St. Joseph.
Society of Saint Edmund Archives, Saint Michael's College, Colchester, VT

Srs. Joan Marshall, Dolores Bachman, and
Marie Albert Alderman wearing the grey
"mission habit," 1968
*Archives of the Sisters of St. Joseph of
Rochester, NY*

Sr. Lorraine Julien instructing
students at Our Lady Queen
of Peace School, ca. 1975
*Archives of the Sisters of St.
Joseph of Rochester, NY*

Most Rev. Joseph
Hogan, Bishop of
Rochester, visiting
Our Lady Queen of
Peace School, 1976
*Archives of the
Sisters of St. Joseph of
Rochester, NY*

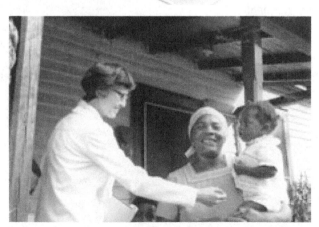

Sr. Mary Weaver visits a family in her work as Assistant Executive Director of the
Selma-Dallas County Community Action Agency, 1984
Society of St. Edmund Archives, Saint Michael's College, Colchester, VT

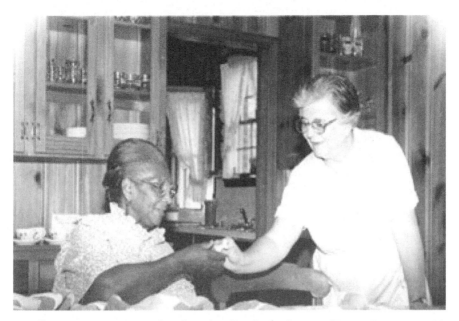

Sr. Albertine Devereaux with a friend at Our Lady Queen of Peace Convent, 1985
Photo by Sr. Beatrice Ganley, SSJ
Archives of the Sisters of St. Joseph of Rochester, NY

Sr. Nancy Clark offers assistance at the Community Center in Pine Apple, 1985
Photo by Sr. Beatrice Ganley, SSJ
Archives of the Sisters of St. Joseph of Rochester, NY

Sr. Maureen Finn, Director of Social Ministry for Our Lady Queen of Peace
Parish, on a home visit, late 1970s
Archives of the Sisters of St. Joseph of Rochester, NY

Sr. Mary Maloy, outreach worker in the Rural Health Medical Program in Pine
Apple, with one of her clients, 1989
Photo by Mary Ellen Potts
Archives of the Sisters of St. Joseph of Rochester, NY

Srs. Anne Urquhart, Shirley Casler, and Josette Capozzi at Our Lady Queen of
Peace Convent, 1990
Archives of the Sisters of St. Joseph of Rochester, NY

Sr. Anne Urquhart with Idella Moore at Our Lady Queen of Peace Parish, 1986
Archives of the Sisters of St. Joseph of Rochester, NY

Kathy Lambert and Sally De Carolis, students from Nazareth Academy in
Rochester, tarpaper a house while doing community service in Selma, 1987
Archives of the Sisters of St. Joseph of Rochester, NY

Sr Josette Capozzi visiting "Mama Willie" Pettway, 1970s
Archives of the Sisters of St. Joseph of Rochester, NY

Sr. Nancy Clark with children at the Pine Apple Learning Center, 1990s
Archives of the Sisters of St. Joseph of Rochester, NY

Sr. Kathleen Navarra and Sr. Patricia Flass at the Pine Apple Community Center,
ca. 1998
Archives of the Sisters of St. Joseph of Rochester, NY

Sr. Kathleen Navarra and Sr. Janet Connorton display the sign for Mary's Food
and Fashion, the gift shop in Pine Apple named in honor of Sr. Mary Maloy in
2000.
Archives of the Sisters of St. Joseph of Rochester, NY

Sr. Kathleen Navarra, who holds a Master Fourth Degree Black Belt, has orga-
nized Korean martial arts classes for at-risk children in Selma, Camden, and
Vredenburgh (2017).
Archives of the Sisters of St. Joseph of Rochester, NY

Sr. Patricia Flass working in the Adult Day Care program in Pine Apple, ca. 1999
Society of Saint Edmund Archives, Saint Michael's College, Colchester, VT

Sr. Donna Del Santo (front right) with students from Nazareth Academy on a community service visit to Selma in 2000.
Archives of the Sisters of St. Joseph of Rochester, NY

Srs. Joan Marshall, Anita Kurowski, and Nancy Clark attending the
fiftieth anniversary commemoration of Bloody Sunday, 2015
Archives of the Sisters of St. Joseph of Rochester, NY

Congressman John Lewis (center), Congresswoman Louise Slaughter (left), and Sisters of St. Joseph who served in Selma posed in front of the Good Samaritan window at the SSJ Motherhouse in Rochester, NY, 2016
Photo by Dave Esposito
Archives of the Sisters of St. Joseph of Rochester, NY

GOOD SAM

There is vigorous testimony in the pages of the annals and correspondence attesting to the paucity of health care available to the Black people of Selma and its hinterlands at the time of the Sisters' arrival in 1940. However, there had been an attempt to build and maintain a hospital that would serve indigent white and Black patients almost 60 years before.

Due to the confluence of several centers of various religious sects in the Selma area in the latter part of the nineteenth century, there was a serious effort to establish a hospital for Selma's sick and indigent (Fitts, 2016, p. 137). Accordingly, a Mrs. Sally Hardee Roy, a member of the local Episcopal Church, called together a group of women to spearhead the project. Dubbed the Society of United Charities, their mission was "to relieve the sick and destitute in and near said city of Selma, irrespective of race, sex, or religion…" (Fitts, ibid.) One of the women donated the land and, under pressure from Mrs. Roy, the city council agreed to help. By the end of 1889, the Charity Hospital and Selma Infirmary tended to the Black and poor of Selma. There were, of course, separate wards for Blacks and whites, but the mission was clearly intended to be a work of charity. Sadly, that hospital closed in 1907, due to the rescinding of support from the male Protestant clergy, and the rise of a number of private hospitals. In its place, that same year, the Burwell Infirmary, Selma's first Black hospital opened, headed by Dr. L.L. Burwell, a Black physician. In 1921, a group of white physicians opened Good Samaritan Hospital and thus, by the 1920's, Selma was the only city in the South to house two Black hospitals, and it is worthy to note that, on Bloody Sunday, March 7, 1965, the Black wounded did not only go to Good Samaritan Hospital for treatment, but they also sought aid at the Burwell Infirmary. In 1971 the Burwell Infirmary ceased operation, leaving only Good Samaritan Hospital to treat the indigent. That same year the Sisters of St. Joseph would withdraw from Good Samaritan hospital.

The "separate but equal" treatment of Black patients was separate but blatantly unequal. When Blacks did visit a clinic, the treatment was of inferior quality, and, with few exceptions, staffed by white doctors who barely observed the "do no harm" promise, and only grudgingly rendered medical attention. Moreover, due to the living conditions of poor Blacks, medical follow-up was sorely lacking, and the inability to purchase prescription medicine or even to travel to medical appointments made it extremely difficult for Black people to recover their health. Finally, the types of food that Black people could afford, and cuisine that was traditional contributed to a variety of diseases and deficiencies.

Several entries in the annals of the mission and various letters attest to the fact that tuberculosis and venereal diseases were most prevalent among the Black community. Added to that, open fires in the houses led to numerous cases of burns, and the lack of safety regulations resulted in horrific work accidents among these working poor. The annals provide ample evidence:

> Sisters Frances Marie and Anastasia visited an old man in the colored hospital. He was dying as a result of severe burns. (Annals, March 13, 1941).

And again:

> About midnight the grandmother woke up in a burning shack. They all left the house and gathered in the yard. Then the grandfather began counting heads. Hardly had he finished his count when he heard a shrill crying sound from within the burning shack.... [H]e dragged [the little girl] to safety and gave her to her mother just before the roof caved in....We couldn't save the grandfather and he died in a few days. The child is getting along well and she will be going home soon to a barn.(Annals from 1947).

It was Sister Anastasia McCormick, one of the original five Sisters in Selma, who brought to the Edmundites' attention the need for a hospice for dying Black people in the parish and its surroundings. Sister Anastasia had been trained as a nurse at St. Joseph's Hospital in Elmira, NY, an institution owned and operated by the Sisters of St. Joseph. She brought with her that rare quality among healthcare givers that combines conscientious concern for the sick and a determination to alleviate the causes of illness.

Recognizing that there was an immediate need for palliative care for the sick and aged, the Inn of the Holy Infant was created in 1943, and the Sisters staffed it. Although it was apparent that this was a real need, the concept had been one of the reasons for the Sisters' presence with the mission. However, Father Casey and the Sisters soon realized that a real hospital was needed. In a letter to Mother Rose Miriam dated April 6, 1944, Sister Anastasia noted:

> In the process of arranging to open the Inn of the Holy Infant two things happened. First in discussing it with Bishop Toolen, he told me of a woman doctor
>
> (Doctor Isabelle Dumont) who was most anxious to take up medical missionary work...Secondly, I talked to one of the local doctors who had hitherto been hostile to our efforts...[I]n talking with him later he brought up the [reason] why he did not do something about helping with a colored hospital. I talked with him about the doctor (Dumont) and told him regardless of the attitude of the medical profession in town I was definitely going to open a clinic and a small hospital of perhaps twelve beds...I was then approached by several doctors in connection with the colored hospital.

There was a question as to who would own a hospital; Father Casey had posed this question in April, 1944. In a letter to Mother Rose Miriam on April 11, 1944, he wrote:

> Do you want me to buy the hospital in the name of your Community or would you rather have it remain with the Diocese? If the former, please send me the correct corporate title. I am starting today in an attempt to buy some property around the hospital and it will save transferring the deeds later on.

It would seem, from later events, that Mother Rose Miriam demurred on owning the hospital, and the Edumundites ended up purchasing it, probably realizing that they would have more control over its operations than if it were owned by the city of Selma.

Finally, both Sister Anastasia and the Edmundites had realized their dream and, seeking financial support for this new endeavor, because the

Edmundites had gone into considerable debt, Sister Anastasia wrote to Father Randall, of the Propagation of the Faith in Rochester in 1944:

> Four years ago the Sisters of St. Joseph from the Rochester diocese were privileged to accept a call to the mission fields of Alabama...Now we are faced with a new responsibility-a hospital for the colored (sic). Into our hands have been placed the lives of these neglected patients, ranging from helpless babes to the feeble aged. In bringing relief to their pain-wracked bodies we shall, God willing, reach their souls to make them pleasing in the sight of God.

In return for benefactors' generosity, she pledged:

> We promise sincerely, Father, that to anyone who will help, we shall give in return all that we possess, our daily prayers and sacrifices...

In reply, Father Randall wrote a letter to several known Catholics who had been generous in the past and asked for their support for Good Samaritan Hospital. Should they not find within their means to make a monetary donation, Father Randall quoted Sister Anastasia: "please pray for our success".

There were, at that time, five hospitals in Selma: three were exclusively for white patients: two were owned and operated by consortia of local doctors, and one was operated by the Baptist church. The two colored hospitals included one, the Burwell Infirmary, owned by a "colored couple". Sister Anastasia wrote (April 6, 1944) "it is the smaller of the two colored hospitals and does not amount to much."

The second of the "colored" hospitals was Good Samaritan, located two blocks from the Sisters' convent. Lest one imagine it as a medical building, the fact is that it consisted of several wooden buildings, decrepit and dirty. It was owned by the doctors who ran the Baptist Hospital., and had been established as Baptist Good Samaritan Hospital in 1922. Although these doctors were white, the Good Samaritan Hospital was exclusively for Black patients. Again, Father Casey, in the same missive described it:

> As far as the usual conception of the hospital goes, it is nothing much either. It is a series of frame buildings added to the original, the latest addition including a small operating room....I am afraid if I described the hospital to you as I found it that you would be

*discouraged from sending Sisters to it. It is not alone the condition
of being overcrowded, it is the general condition of the whole place.*

Surprisingly, there were no laundry facilities, and open fireplaces, burn-
ing wood or coal provided the only heat. There were very few toilets or bath
facilities and no hot water tanks. There were so few eating utensils, patients
had to eat with their fingers. Mattresses were infested with vermin and bed
linen was scarce. Nurses and aides worked 12-hour days for a weekly salary
of $3.00. (Wall, 2009). In short, the newly acquired hospital was hardly a
place to get well.

The hospital, established in 1922, under the aegis of the Baptist church
and the ownership of a group of white doctors, struggled through World
War II, and in 1944, when the Edmudites bought it, they borrowed a total
of $82,000 and then contacted their benefactors in the North to help them
pay for it. Father Casey was very worried about the staffing of the hospital,
and even before the bill of sale was finalized, wrote to Mother Rose Miriam
to secure three Sisters to staff the hospital. He wrote to Mother Rose Miriam on March 25, 1944:

> *I have had to stop negotiations until I can find Sisters. My first
> choice is the Sisters of St. Joseph, since there will be a close connec-
> tion with the Inn of the Holy Infant and eventually the two will
> become one institution. I do not like to mix the Sisters.*

He then went on to mention that, if Mother Rose Miriam refused to
send Sisters, he would have to make an offer to the Sisters of Mercy.

It must have worked. The annals of April 10, 1944 read thus:

Telegram from Nazareth telling of Sisters coming for hospital.

On June 1, 1944, the Edmundites had finalized their negotiations and
took over the ownership of the hospital.

In an interview taped in 1971, Sister Frances Marie set the scene, as they
visited Good Samaritan Hospital for the first time:

> *When we went into the operating room, just above the operat-
> ing table was dirt hanging down from the ceiling. Sister Anastasia
> quickly got to work cleaning and fixing it up. When we needed
> additional help, we drove to the street corners where unemployed
> colored men gathered. Since we had no money to pay them, we*

promised them clothes from the clothing room in exchange for their
labor. We had many takers.

Sister Anastasia had her own agenda when she arrived in 1940. While the other Sisters might be assessing the possibility of opening a school, Sister Anastasia focused on the healthcare needs of those she visited. She encouraged the Edmundites to purchase the Good Samaritan Hospital from the doctors, since a hospital was definitely in the Edmundites' plans for the Selma mission, (Wall, 2009) and Sister Anastasia had been sent to Selma to help them to realize the operation of a hospital for Black patients, one that would not condescend to their needs, but would treat Black patients with dignity and care.

In 1945, after lengthy negotiations, the Edmundite mission finalized the purchase of Good Samaritan Hospital, and the Sisters set about making it habitable. The Holy Infant Inn for the elderly was soon connected to the newly acquired hospital so that there could be a sufficient continuum of care for the sick elderly. The first few weeks, in addition to dealing with the pervasive filth of the place, the Sisters also had to deal with a vermin infestation. Sister Louis Bertrand, the first administrator after the departure of Sister Anastasia observed:

The mattresses had more life in them than some of the patients.
We took them out and burned them. (the mattresses, not the patients)

If there had been any doubts as to the need for a Black hospital, it became apparent early on that the harvest would be great. In a letter to Mother Rose Miriam a year after the hospital had been acquired, Sister Louis Bertrand, who arrived after the departure of Sister Anastasia, wrote (November 10, 1946):

The increase in patients keeps our beds full all the time and we
frequently have two in a bed. A year ago such an idea of two pa-
tients in one bed was very far from my mind. But now that I am
starting my second year in Selma many unusual things see quite
natural now.

With the eventual complicity of a few white doctors, Sister nurses got busy creating a hospital worthy of its clientele.

Words cannot describe the work of Sister Anastasia in bringing about Good Samaritan Hospital as a real place for the Black people of Selma to receive quality medical care. Her indomitable energy in hands-on work-scrubbing floors and walls, carrying out vermin-filled mattresses, begging, borrowing or confiscating furnishings in order to make first the Holy Infant Inn habitable and then Good Samaritan Hospital is nothing short of heroic. While working incessantly, she suffered several physical ailments of her own, but did not let her own personal discomfort interfere with her vision. Sister Anastasia McCormick left Selma in December, 1944, to be replaced by Sister Anna Patricia Barry, a registered nurse.

Sister Louis Bertrand, the hospital's first Sister administrator, arrived the following year, in 1945, and spent the next twenty years growing the hospital, from a series of lowly wood frame houses, to a modern facility in 1964 that was the envy of Blacks and whites in the South, and the only Black hospital in a six-county area. "Louie B" as she was affectionately known by the Sisters, was a whirlwind of energy. She was a rather rotund woman, and prone to causing considerable anxiety whenever she landed on a rickety piece of furniture. Once, during Mass at the convent, the chair in which she was seated collapsed, sending the two altar boys, students in the school, into fits of hilarity. She took it in good humor, and won the affection of said altar boys, when she appeared in school later in the day and beamed at the two boys.

Sister Louis Bertrand Dixon was 41 years old when she arrived in Selma to head the hospital. She had acquired a Bachelor's degree in nursing in 1936 from the Catholic University of America, and had served as both a nurse and a nurse instructor at St. Joseph's Hospital in Elmira. Although she had several health issues that would plague her over the nineteen years that she worked in Selma, rarely did she let her illnesses curtail her energetic style. Even her serious automobile accident in February of 1963 failed to diminish her zeal. Instead, she planned and executed the building of the modern hospital, several additions to the building, and, of course, the school of practical nursing. She only left Selma in 1964 because her failing health prevented her from staying even longer.

But Good Samaritan hospital did not appear full-blown; over the years it was upgraded and improved so that, twenty years after its acquisition, it was a modern 4-storey structure. In between, after the efforts of Sister Anastasia to acquire the hospital, Sister Louis Bertrand's nineteen-year tenure gradually developed it. Two years after her arrival, in 1947, she oversaw a brick extension of the hospital, and ten years later, a second extension that included an extended care facility. By December 21, 1964 there was a structure and facility that housed the only hospital for Blacks in six counties.

In a 1958 interview with *The Colored Harvest,* a publication of the Josephite Missionaries, Sister Louis Bertrand outlined the challenges and steps that led to her creating a functioning, clean, and welcoming Good Samaritan Hospital:

> *There weren't enough trained nurses to care for the patients and no wonder! The few nurses available were on duty twelve hours a day for three dollars a week. The result? The patients were woefully neglected while the attendants were usually sitting in the sun. No one cared what happened to the sick. If they died, it was not unexpected; if they got well, it was another extraordinary proof of human endurance.*
>
> *Occasionally a doctor came to the hospital to perform an operation, Imagine that sight! The poorly lighted, stuffy room, the filthy floor, and half-clean equipment, while the doctor operated with his hat and coat on. Why the note of dignity? Simply because he was afraid to lay his clothes down-they would be crawling with bugs and vermin by the time he'd leave. (The Colored Harvest, May, 1958, pp.12-14.)*

Through that period of growth that included, in 1950, the School of Practical Nursing, Sister Louis Bertrand personally birthed this effort not only to maintain a supply of nurses, but to provide a professional path for Black men and women. She kept Mother Helene apprised of every step and upgrade:

> *The little chapel has undergone many changes. A floor has been put in and it has been painted...and we installed peach drapes. Each room has an exhaust ceiling fan...There is a hydraulic lift, special wheel chairs, and special walkers. The little servicing kitch-*

en is yellow with white and black tile walls…(Letter to Mother He-
lene, December 29, 1957).

Sister Louis Bertrand became the recipient of urgent care herself when
she suffered a serious car accident in February, 1963. Sister Liguori, who
was with Sister Louis Bertrand, and was herself injured, reported, in the
Selma Times-Journal of November 22, 1964, that Sister Louis Bertrand had
had to return to Rochester for convalescence and rehabilitation. Sister
Barbara Lum recalls:

Sister Mary Paul, Margaret and I hurried to Selma Baptist
Hospital, because Sister Louis Bertrand appeared to be dying. She
eventually rallied after several transfusions. (Interview with Sister
Barbara Lum, December 26, 2020).

The new hospital opened in her absence, but her spirit was certainly
present. The article concluded: 'The new Good Samaritan Hospital em-
bodies many of Sister Louis Bertrand's ideas and suggestions and will be a
living monument to her service.'

Since one of the most frequent causes of medical attention was burns,
Sister Louis Bertrand opened a burn unit. Letters to Rochester described
the situation:

Some children came to the hospital with arms or legs burned off
and faces horribly burned.

Sister Barbara Lum, who worked in pediatric nursing from 1959 to 1968
also recalls:

By far the most frequent reason for children's hospital stays was
burns. The houses often had open fires and children would either
fall into the fires, or harm themselves playing in the fires. We had
a five-year-old girl who was brought in with extensive burns, and
she had to stay in the hospital for several months because she need-
ed skin grafts. I will never forget: she would sit straight up in the
gurney as she was being brought to the operating room, because she
didn't want to miss a thing. During her stay, I occupied her with
little jobs so that she felt needed and happy to be doing something.
(Interview with Sister Barbara Lum, December 26, 2020)

Children with cleft palates, cleft lips, club feet, and other disabilities showed up too. An 18-year-old showed up with tuberculosis of the spine. She weighed 70 pounds and wore a heavy body cast. Another patient had a very deep wound to his arm from an errant axe. Many came seeking treatment from beatings from the local Ku Klux Klan. Though they had no means of paying the cost of medical care, many patients offered to work in the hospital to pay off their bills. If one wished to behold the visage of poverty and racism, Good Samaritan Hospital was the place to do it.

The hospital, though it treated its share of misery, also provided to Black children and the aged a modicum of joy. Sister Louis Bertrand wrote to Mother Helene to describe the Christmas celebration:

> Santa visited the children and old folks at the hospital. The old people were a sight to see. The first thing they did was to eat their candy. James received a red shirt and he has not had it off since. Aunt Mary-age 93-was found later in the day applying her toothpaste to her feet. She thought it was something for her rheumatism. Old Ben felt sorry because I did not have a package so he offered me a pair of his blue socks. (Letter to Mother Helene, December 29, 1957).

When Sister Louis Bertrand passed away on December 11, 1974, her obituary quoted her friend, Sister Liguori:

> During all this time, she was an able administrator, a trusted friend, and counselor to many who worked with her, devoted to the sick whom she visited daily, and a source of strength and courage to all who came to her.

The hospital, notable for its mission of caring for the sick poor in a Catholic setting, would become legendary for three significant events: the establishment of a school of practical nursing, the involvement of Dr. Isabel Dumont and Miss Joan Mulder, and the role of the Sisters at the hospital on March 7, 1965, to be later known as "Bloody Sunday".

THE NURSING SCHOOL

TRAINED nurses and aides were constantly in short supply. Many white nurses refused to work in a Black hospital, and the education system for Blacks was so lacking, that Black nurses were nowhere to be found. And so, in 1950, Sister Louis Bertrand Dixon established a school for practical nursing-the very first in Alabama. Although the school was open to students regardless of color, or creed, the vast majority of students were Black and non-Catholic and female. It is important to note that a recurring theme surrounded the work of the Sisters: the education and betterment of the lives of Black women. Upon arriving in Selma, Sister Frances Marie had commented on the need for the education of the women in the parish. The fact that the Sisters had founded two girls' high schools and a women's college in Rochester is testament to their dedication to the realization of the potential of women, and so the establishment of the school of practical nursing was not inconsistent with this dedication.

Though criticized for not providing a school for registered nurse training, it is important to note that, several times in the years after their arrival in 1940, the Sisters had visited the Tuskegee Institute (Annals for May 3, 1941). They met with founder Booker T. Washington only once, but made several trips to the Institute and invested in Washington's philosophy that Black people needed to focus on the practical issues of life, and to take care of immediate needs first. In addition to this observation, it should be noted that Black children rarely attended or even finished high school. Later on, Sister Mary Christopher Kuchman, who eventually took over the operation of the nursing school, added a General Equivalency Diploma (GED) program to the school so that nursing students would have a high school diploma.

Apparently, the creation of a school of practical nursing was not the first item on the agenda. Father Lambert wrote to Mother Rose Miriam one year before the nursing school opened:

> We also talked of our desire to initiate the first year of a high school. You did not know whether you would have a Sister to spare for such a program. However, you did promise to advise me by the middle of the summer whether or not you could see your way clear to it. That would give us sufficient time to make all necessary arrangements. I will, of course, anxiously await your answer and in the meantime will say a solemn prayer that it will be favorable. (Letter to Mother Rose Miriam, June 20, 1949).

It is important to note that, with the opening of the school of nursing, the hospital did not hire any dedicated instructors, with the exception of *ad hoc* guest lecturers. Instead, the Sisters, besides having regular rounds and a full nursing duty, also taught in the school of nursing. Although this must have been a brutal schedule, the Sisters were able to use their experience with this particular population, their knowledge of the extreme circumstances of their patients, and familiarity with the maladies of poor people to provide a unique training for their students.

The plan was to enroll twenty to forty students annually, and applicants had to have at least eight years of grammar school. Since attendance at a high school was rare, priority was given to any applicant who had had at least one year in high school. The students had no living facilities attached to the hospital, so they sought the magnanimous hospitality of local Black families.

The school did more than provide professional training for these nurses in training. The brochure for the new nursing school stated as its mission: "To prepare professional women, equipped physically, intellectually, and spiritually, to provide self-satisfaction and community welfare." Note that nowhere in the mission statement does care for the sick and dying appear; the target of this endeavor was the Black women of the South. The compassionate care they evidenced was collateral benefit, as the brochure continued: "under the guidance of Religion and Catholic Philosophy" the applicants would "develop a Christ-like spirit toward the sick". (Brochure, Good Samaritan School of Practical Nursing, SSJ Archives)

If one were to visit the little Selma History Museum, one would see a photo of a group of proud-looking Black women; they are the first graduates of the Good Samaritan School of Practical Nursing. Of note is Etta Perkins, to this day a well-dressed, energetic octogenarian who plays cards at the Edmundite Center every week. She proudly identifies herself and states: "Good Samaritan opened the doors for us all" (*Interview with Etta Perkins December 6, 2019*). Ms Perkins went on to become a registered nurse and taught classes at Good Samaritan, and her son became the first Black mayor of Selma-open doors indeed!

The Sisters conducted classes that included theory and practicum. Sister

Mary Christopher Kuchman was a trained registered nurse and she recalls:

I was sent to Selma in 1964 during the race riots in Rochester. I always wanted to be a missionary, but I wanted to be a Mary-knoll Sister. I was teaching in the hospital in Elmira and was sent to Alabama right after the nursing school graduates left. I don't remember much about my reception in Alabama, but I was sent right to Good Sam.

I worked in the pharmacy, and soon after my arrival, Sister Michael Ann (who replaced Sister Louis Bertrand) came in and said, 'I want you to take over the management of the nursing school two days from now.' All I know is the Holy Spirit took over and I took on the running of the practical nursing program, about which I knew nothing.

I went to Montgomery to inquire about the status of the school of nursing and the gentleman in the accreditation office told me that they intended to close the Good Samaritan program because the students were not well prepared. So I did whatever was needed to save the school.

I put together a curriculum, and started keeping several note-books to create a real sense of quality for the nursing school. I knew that we had to go through an accreditation by the state of Alabama and so I started working on that.

A gentleman came from Montgomery and started asking questions. I showed him my notebooks and he said, 'I have never seen anything like this.' He wanted to grant us immediate accreditation, but I wanted to work harder at it.

When Sister Evelyn Connelly replaced Sister Michael Ann as administrator of the hospital, she told me that she was going to eliminate the obstetrics department. I knew that our nursing students needed their rotation in that area for their preparation, so I took them every week to the white hospital in Montgomery. That's how we got accreditation and provided a complete preparation for our nursing students. (Interview with Sister Mary Christopher Kuchman, May 17, 2021)

As she celebrated her sixtieth anniversary as a Sister of St. Joseph, the *Finger Lakes Times* (October 7, 2007) ran a laudatory article about Sister Mary Christopher, who, by that time, was working in Waterloo, NY. She affirmed the core purpose of the Good Samaritan nursing program:

I loved my 6 ½ years at Good Samaritan. I felt I was doing God's work and making a difference in those girls' lives, giving them a chance to lift themselves up by being nurses.

After the events of March 7, 1965, Sister Electa (Carol Spada) then a Sister of St. Joseph of Rochester, came to Selma to take the Licensed Practical Nurse Program at Good Samaritan. Etta Perkins was one of her teachers, and named her third child Syethia Electa, after Sister Electa.

By 1966, Good Samaritan School of Practical Nursing had graduated over 300 students. This provided personnel for the hospital, and, in the wake of Civil Rights legislation of the 1960's, meant that Black professionals had an avenue to decent living wages and, even more important, self-determination.

That same year, Sisters Michael Ann Hanley and Eleanor (Barbara Lum) attended the Alabama Hospital Association Public Education Committee meeting. Having secured permission to treat Medicare patients, the Sisters needed training in taking care of these patients. In July of that year, Sister Michael Ann, now the administrator of Good Samaritan Hospital, was appointed to the selfsame Public Education Committee, and to the Dallas County Chamber of Commerce. This was the first time that a Sister from Good Samaritan Hospital was asked to serve on these important bodies, despite the fact that Good Samaritan had been a stalwart member of the Selma community for twenty-three years.

It is worth noting that the original intent in the foundation of the mission in 1940 was the conversion of Black people to the Catholic faith. Although the Sisters had been relieved, in 1946, of their catechizing duties, the hospital, as well as the school, provided a milieu in which the Catholic faith could flourish and spread. In 1959 alone, the Sisters recorded in baptisms 41 infants, 15 children, 8 adults, and 10 stillborn infants.(Analysis of Hospital Service, 1959).

DR. ISABEL DUMONT AND MISS JOAN MULDER

No account of the story of Good Samaritan Hospital nor the management of health care among the Black residents of Selma would be complete without mention of two women who made an indelible mark on Selma's history and colluded with the Sisters in several ways.

Doctor Isabel Dumont and Joan Mulder were two women who met in unlikely circumstances, became life-long friends and collaborators, and dedicated their lives to the Black people of Selma.

Isabel Dumont was born in Cologne, Germany in 1908. In 1932, she received an exchange scholarship to study at St. Catherine College in St. Paul, Minnesota, and completed her undergraduate degree in 1936. After getting her Medical Doctor degree from Women's Medical College , she interned in Philadelphia, Pennsylvania. In 1938, while doing post-doctoral work at Trinity College In Washington, DC, she met Joan Mulder, a native of Deventer, Netherlands. Having received a bachelor's degree in biology from Trinity, Joan Mulder was eager to travel to Africa to do health care work among the Africans. It just so happened that Dr. Dumont had the same desire.

With the war putting those plans on hold, both women traveled to St. Vincent's Hospital in Birmingham, Alabama where they met Bishop Toolen and told him of their desire to work in Africa. "Africa!" Toolen exclaimed, "How can you think of going to Africa, when Selma is only a hundred miles away?"(*The Catholic Week*, May 24, 1985, article on the commemoration of the death of Dr. Dumont)

And so they contacted the Edmundites, who had just purchased Good Samaritan Hospital, and set up a clinic on September 8, 1944. Eventually, Dr. Dumont would also set up a pediatric and maternity clinic; that meant that she worked in two clinics and the hospital. The *Catholic Week* for May 24, 1985 reported that "for years Dr. Dumont was the only doctor on call at 'Good Sam' delivering thousands of babies and performing hundreds of emergency operations." Until she died in 1985, Dr. Dumont gave 41 years of her life to the Black people of Selma, enduring threats from the KKK, lack of funds and resources, and, often, the odium of white residents of Selma. Both she and Ms Mulder received Papal medals in recognition of their work for the Edmundite missions in 1961.

Sister Barbara Lum remembers Dr. Dumont and Ms. Mulder:

> They were quite the characters. They loved the Sisters and they loved their patients. But they certainly let you know when they didn't like something, and they also let you know when they did like something. (Interview with Sister Barbara Lum, December 26, 2020)

Both Dr. Dumont and Ms Mulder interacted with the Sisters on a social level. Several times in the annals is mention of the Sisters' being hosted at parties and dinners either at the women's residence, the Tally Ho restaurant, which is still in business (2021), or at their cottage on Lake Mitchell. The Sisters were able to spend vacation days at said cottage as guests of Dumont and Mulder, and, in turn, made the women welcome at various jubilee, birthday, and feast day celebrations. Thus the women were integrated into the supportive community that included the Edmundites, the Sisters, and these gracious, generous women.

When Dr. Dumont died, the Mobile Diocesan newspaper for May 24, 1985 declared, "Selma has lost a saint". Sister Elizabeth LeValley, superior of the Sisters of St. Joseph at the time, wrote to Joan Mulder:

> Dear Joan: my sympathy to you. My gratitude that I met Dr. Dumont twice and was moved by the strength of her spirit. We will make a donation to the mission in her name. (Telegram from Sisters of St. Joseph to Joan Mulder May 21, 1985)

A Mercy Sister, Mary Margaret Durick, from Mobile, attended the funeral of Dr. Dumont and described it in a letter :

> She was laid out in the Edmundite Memorial Chapel in a beautiful lime colored dress. The blanket of flowers on the casket was from her brother Edmundites. ...the church was filled to capacity... Sisters read, a beautiful black man led the singing...[Sisters] Mary Weaver and Jane Kelly brought up gifts. Father Leary gave a beautiful homily-who is my neighbor: Said if we could only get out of the way and let God take over!

Joan Mulder worked and lived with Dr. Dumont for those 41 years serving as lab assistant, X-ray technician and medical technologist. She was also an accomplished artist and established the Canterbury Art Guild in 1947 to encourage budding artists. Both she and Dr. Dumont established a chapter of Alcoholics Anonymous and a venereal disease clinic after the state of Alabama mandated treatment for venereal disease for every state citizen, and, in 1949, formed a Nurses' Club at Good Samaritan Hospital. Despite the national and international honors both she and Dr. Dumont received, the one that mattered most was a party from the people of Selma honoring Ms Mulder and Dr. Dumont in 1978.

Joan Mulder died less than a year after her life-long friend had passed away. On November 21, 1986, the *Birmingham News* led the notice with this headline: "Joan Mulder's life was one of love for others." At her death it was revealed that she had mentored and supported countless young Black boys and girls in their pursuit of their own dreams. Sister Mary Weaver, who had come to Selma in 1964, noted: "She was just a spark of light in everybody's life."

In 1989, some of the Sisters moved into the house on Griffin Street that had been occupied by Dr. Dumont and Miss Mulder during their many years in Selma.

GOOD SAMARITAN ON THE MAP: BLOODY SUNDAY AND ITS AFTERMATH
As has been noted previously, the Sisters who arrived in Selma in September of 1940 were the product of their time. They scoffed at any hint that integration of black and white people might actually happen. Their mission was to assess the needs, teach the word of God, baptize babies and adults, and relieve the suffering of Black people in the South. Both the culture of the South and the opinion of the Catholic Church were set on "separate but equal" business as usual. The tide of history and the implacable movements fostered during the decade of the 1960's would not bypass Selma, Alabama, however. The involvement of Good Samaritan hospital and the Sisters who worked there was more than anyone could have foreseen and would have a series of consequences that would transform the Sisters' involvement in the Selma mission, the role of Catholic women religious in social justice movements, and the nature of their ministry. Due to powerful forces that would soon be felt, both St. Elizabeth School, as has been described above,

and Good Samaritan Hospital faced a shortage of days in their existence.

The struggle for civil rights and equality of Blacks was not new to Selma, but various groups such as the Southern Christian Leadership Conference, led by Rev. Martin Luther King, and the Student Non-Violent Coordinating Committee (SNCC) led by John Lewis, and other groups both in Black and white communities coalesced during the first years of the 1960's to demand legislation that would guarantee economic and civic equality. For the first time, the support for these causes was not only coordinated, but was taken up by widespread support from a huge segment of the American populace.

The city of Selma was hardly a blip on the radar of the civil rights movement, even though several demonstrations for voting rights had been staged there. However, an event just prior to making Selma a flashpoint and the focus of people who didn't even know Selma existed precipitated a series of moves that would make "Selma" and "civil rights" synonymous.

The increasing number of "Freedom Riders" from the North brought attention to the lack of voting rights among Blacks, despite the wording of the fifteenth amendment to the Constitution. The white people of Selma chafed under the introduction of "outside agitators" from the North. Specifically, though Blacks made up over 50% of Selma's population, only 2% of them were registered to vote. Poll taxes, so-called literacy tests, and harassment from the Klan discouraged Black people from even trying to register, let alone vote.

The Sisters, always treading a fine line between the world of Black people and the white world, knew that discrimination in the South existed; after all, Sisters had been in Selma for 25 years by then. Accordingly, they boycotted grocery stores in Selma and shopped up in Montgomery instead. On one occasion, while waiting in line to buy ice cream, Sisters Josepha Twomey, Barbara Lum, and Loretta Poole left the premises when they saw that Black patrons were refused service (Interview April 11, 2008).

Although the so-called "Bloody Sunday" of March 7, 1965 has claimed its rightful amount of attention, this event was not an isolated one. Events leading up to the march had been piling up, as voter registration drives in Selma increased. Sister Mary Paul wrote an extensive missive on February

7, 1965, exactly one month before "Bloody Sunday". In it, she described the
various occurrences that were happening all around the Sisters. Her letter
sought to clarify for those in the North what they were reading in their
daily newspaper:

> *Lest there should be any misunderstanding from the beginning,
> let me emphasize two things very clearly: in one message something
> was said about the Sisters and Fathers being neutral. ...we are
> most definitely NOT(sic) neutral. For all practical purposes, we are
> "negroes"(sic) living in a Negro community. The second thing that
> needs to be clarified is this. One Sister writing, after seeing Mrs.
> Cooper strike Sheriff Clark, was concerned that such a woman
> would do the same thing to us. ...We are in no danger whatsoever.
> (Letter of Sister Mary Paul Geck to friends and family, February
> 7, 1965).*

Sister Mary Paul stressed the nonviolent character of the efforts of Black
citizens to register to vote: "*The thing that impresses me so much is that in
the midst of all this turmoil, the people never lose their sense of humor.*"

She goes on to describe, in gritty detail, the string of arrests made by
Sheriff Jim Clark, the county sheriff's deputies and the Selma police. Most
galling is the arrest of school children; many were students at St. Elizabeth
School where Sister Mary Paul was the principal:

> *On Monday two of the 8th graders did not come. Tuesday it was
> four, Wednesday six and by Friday I was minus eleven. By Friday
> there were so many confined that an announcement was made that
> parents should just go and pick up their children either from the
> armory or from Camp Selma (10 miles outside of Selma).*

As if to presage the events that would occur just one month later, Sister
Mary Paul eloquently predicted:

> *The marches on the courthouse will continue, and must, until
> the unjust inequalities are rectified. This is the quiet determina-
> tion of the people and one with which we are in full agreement. To
> say or even to hope that it will be done quickly would be foolish
> and blind thinking. It will not be. There will be much sacrifice and
> much hardship before anything is really accomplished. (Letter of*

Sister Mary Paul Geck to the Sisters of St. Joseph of Rochester, February 7, 1965)

Sister Mary Paul came to Selma in 1962 to serve as principal and seventh and eighth grade teacher at St. Elizabeth School. At. Age 44, she already had an impressive record as a teacher in the Diocese of Rochester. In that same letter she chronicled the incidents in which the white government of Selma and Dallas County opposed the civil rights efforts. For example, attempting to visit the teenagers who had been arrested, she and others were met with resistance and obfuscation at every turn. But throughout this impassioned letter, Sister acknowledges and outlines the tensions and energies being brought to bear on Selma. The reader, being well aware of the subsequent events, can easily trace the elements that would come together the next month.

Finally, Sister echoes the fortitude and outright grit that characterized the first Sisters who had arrived a quarter century before:

I think this is a wonderful time to be in Selma. I wouldn't miss it for the world. God love y'all.

The voter rights movement soon entangled the Sisters at Good Samaritan Hospital. Sister Barbara Lum wrote to her parents on October 20, 1963:

Sister Barbara Lum, then known as Sister Eleanor, was a newly-minted registered nurse, a graduate of Nazareth College, when she was assigned to Selma and to Good Samaritan Hospital. Besides her nursing duties, she also taught in the school of practical nursing. Much of what is known about the hospital's role in the March 7, 1965 events and the aftermath, can be attributed to Sister Barbara's letters to her parents and family. Written in Catholic school cursive, they relay not only the day-to-day events experienced by Sister Barbara, but also her own musings on the impact of those events.

In a letter to her parents dated October 20, 1963, Sister Barbara melded the mundane with the profound:

Dear Mom and Dad, Thank you for the wedding pictures of Mary Ann and Pat...Bill said you and he met, both on your way to Johnson's Bakery to buy him cookies. ...This is my last night duty for a while. I have relieved for five weekends, first for Sally's then

Lula's vacation. It is 5:30 AM. I was trying to prepare some classes and a test, but got too sleepy. Now I must go and check the patients again. It has been a very quiet night.

She continues:

Martin Luther King spoke at a mass meeting last Monday. The meeting was over in 45 minutes but Etta Perkins said his talk was the best anyone has given. The next morning began a period of voter registration…The Negro leaders tried to get this broadcast on the radio stations, but they refused. Consequently not too many knew, but the word spread.

Among those who didn't know was your daughter. I had a trip to the Health Department planned for the students (of the nursing school) but they must have thought Sister Electa and I were leading the group to register. A movie cameraman rushed up to get a close up picture and six blue helmeted deputies cum down the court-house steps. I don't know what else happened because I got into the Health Department as fast as I could. We had a good tour and talks and then I had the students go out to the cars six at a time so no one would be standing on the street. I felt like I was timing six or seven getaways. The police followed Mary Towns' car back to the hospital but there was no trouble.

But it was the death of Jimmie Lee Jackson that focused the attention of the civil rights leaders on Selma, and finally touched off the events whose prequel had been described so eloquently by Sister Mary Paul. On the night of February 18, 1965, a group of marchers organized a demonstration in nearby Marion, Alabama. Beset upon by state troopers, Jimmie Lee and his mother fled to a café, where he was shot by a trooper. Because Good Samaritan was one of only two hospitals to which he could be taken, he arrived in bad shape. Even after a hastily arranged surgery, made all the worse because Sister St. Joseph Creighton, the nurse anesthetist was unable to be present, a dentist was called in to administer the anesthesia. Jimmie Lee lingered for a week before succumbing to his injuries. Sister Barbara Lum attended to him, and, as he died, Jimmie Lee said to her, "Don't you think this is a high price for freedom?"

Although there had been demonstrations demanding voting rights, they had started to become more widespread all over the Deep South. But the death of Jimmie Lee Jackson was the spark that the coalition of Black leaders needed to focus on Selma and on the state of Alabama. While Martin Luther King Jr. did not attend the march slated for March 7, 1965, his aide, Hosea Williams and SNCC coordinator John Lewis gathered some 600 people to cross the Edmund Pettis Bridge (named after a local Confederate general) from Selma to the state capital, Montgomery. There the marchers (all Black) would demonstrate outside the state house to demand voting rights. They did not achieve their goal on that Sunday; they achieved much more.

Bishop Toolen had let the religious men and women working in his diocese know that they would not be allowed to take part in the march. Father Oulett, the Edmundite pastor at Queen of Peace Church, noted: "Bishop Toolen told us, 'if you participate in this march, you will be on the first train out of here'" (*Sisters of Selma, 2007*).

Sister Barbara Lum recalls that Sister Josepha Twomey wanted very much to oppose Bishop Toolen's order and she was eager to join meetings and marches that were being organized in the Selma area. But the other Sisters convinced her that the ejection from Selma by the Bishop would be worse; they would be unable to carry on their important ministries. (Interview with Sister Barbara Lum, December 26, 2020).

Bishop Toolen's orders were not to be taken lightly. Father Maurice Oullet, SSE, pastor of St. Elizabeth Parish found this out the hard way. After he allowed the so-called "freedom riders" to use his church as a meeting place, he became more and more involved in the protests. In September, 1963, he and a number of Black Protestant ministers approached Selma's mayor Chris Heinz with a petition to create a bi-racial committee to discuss Black grievances. This was met with stern opposition and went nowhere.

Father Oulett was, in that same month, summoned before a local judge and reprimanded for his activities (Fitts, 2016, p. 240). On April 7, 1965, a month after the Selma to Montgomery march, Bishop Toolen expelled Father Oulett from Alabama, explaining, "I don't want a dead priest on my hands". (Fitts, 2016, p. 256)

As the marchers approached the Edmund Pettis Bridge, which spans the Alabama River, they were met by a phalanx of Sheriff Jim Clark's deputies and Governor George Wallace's state troopers. Using billy clubs and tear gas, the deputies and troopers waded into the line of marchers, or charged them with horses. The marchers never had a chance.

On duty at Good Samaritan Hospital later that day, Sister Barbara Lum went early that Sunday morning to prepare a first aid kit for the marchers, "just in case". She remembers:

> I fixed up a kit, thinking that the worst thing that could happen would be a marcher twisting an ankle or needing an aspirin or something. It was kind of a sunny, windy day, so I put something in the kit for windburn. I just had no idea what was about to happen. (The Bridge, Summer 2000)

Sister Barbara returned to the convent and then heard on the radio that the march had turned violent:

> I just ran. We all just wanted to get over there [to the hospital]. People were in shock. They were just in shock that the march had turned violent. We set up a triage. We said these people need to be stitched up; these patients need to be registered for evaluation, and these have head wounds. (the Bridge, Summer 2000)

Sister Barbara was not the only Sister who ministered to the injured. Sister Liguori Dunlea was 59 years old at the time. She had become a registered nurse in 1927, and eventually became a nursing supervisor at St. Joseph's, and received her bachelor's degree in nursing from the Catholic University of America. She had arrived in Selma in 1961.

Sister Liguori was seriously injured in the 1963 car accident with Sister Louis Bertrand, and after that had a very hard time walking and standing. Of that Sunday she remembers:

> We were relaxing in the community room, when we heard sirens going past. In just a moment, Sister Michael Ann Hanley, administrator of the hospital, called and asked Sister Mary Paul (Geck), who was principal of St. Elizabeth School, and superior of the convent, to have all the sisters come over immediately. (The Bridge, Summer 2000).

She continued:

> We came in and quickly received our assignments. Sister Mary
> Paul was to man an admission desk set up right near the emer-
> gency room. . Sisters St. Joseph, Margaret Isabelle, Mary Christo-
> pher, and Eleanor (Barbara Lum) took care of victims in the dining
> room, set up as a second ER.
>
> Sisters Bernice, Josepha and Felicitas (Mary Weaver) were in-
> valuable in the assistance which they gave in helping transport
> victims to X-ray or a bed, and giving strength and support to the
> suffering victims and their relatives.
>
> The sight was not a pretty one. The injuries included severe head
> lacerations, cuts and bruises, as well as fractures of ankles caused
> by officers' horses trampling on these poor victims. We cared for
> well over 100 victims.

Sister Mary Christopher rushed to duty at the hospital and was appalled:

> It was awful. Those people were beaten so badly by the police.
> We worked very hard to treat them. All the time I was wondering
> how people could do that to people marching for basic rights. (In-
> terview, Finger Lakes Times, October 7, 2007)

Sister Liguori remembers that that Sunday was only the beginning; "We
would continue without respite for the month and beyond." Besides tending to the wounded, the Sisters accommodated the many women religious
who came from all over the country to witness to the effort. A lasting effect
of that effort was an enduring friendship between the Sisters of St. Joseph
and SNCC president, John Lewis, a future Congressman, who suffered a
severe concussion that Sunday afternoon. Similarly, the mission church
of St. Elizabeth was to play host to thousands of Catholics from all over
the country. Sister Mary Paul Geck recalled efforts to accommodate the
throng:

> We realized that we would not have enough Communion hosts
> to accommodate everyone, so I got on the phone to parishes in
> Birmingham and Montgomery to solicit extra hosts. Some priests
> refused outright to supply the mission. Eventually, a group of Car-
> melite Sisters in Montgomery gave the mission a number of large

hosts, which they broke into smaller pieces. (Hite, 2002, p. 328)

A footnote to that day: While the assault was taking place on the Edmund Pettis Bridge, Father Crowley, head of the Edmundite missions, was traveling on a fundraising mission for Good Samaritan Hospital and the Edmundite mission. The hospital was facing a $50,000 deficit (after the events of "Bloody Sunday, that deficit would grow to $102,000), and he had an appointment to meet with Cardinal Francis Spellman, Archbishop of New York. The two men discussed the situation regarding the hospital, as well as the situation in Selma. Spellman wrote a check for $5,000 and asked Father Crowley to read a letter he was having pastors read in all parishes the following Sunday. After the march, the Cardinal added a check for $10,000. (Hite, 2000, p.323).

The marches, including the eventual successful march from Selma to Montgomery resulted in landmark legislation allowing Black people the same right to suffrage as white people. The "Bloody Sunday" and its aftermath had a profound effect on the Sisters of St. Joseph who ministered in Selma, but it had a much more lasting effect on women religious in general. Sister Liguori Dunlea recalled, 35 years later:

In 1965, President Johnson signed the Voting Rights Bill, which provided for the registration of all eligible American citizens. However, like everything else for the Southern Negro, voter registration proceeded at a snail's pace until the federal government sent registrars into the Deep South to assure voter rights. (The Bridge, Summer 2000)

The world had watched as the heroic work of the Sisters provided for the injured marchers. As a result of their ministrations, over three hundred demonstrators were housed, fed, and given respite in the ensuing weeks. President Johnson commended the Sisters, and Connecticut Senator Thomas Dodd, read into the *Congressional Record*:

[Good Samaritan] Hospital has figured predominantly in the news of the last ten days, because it provided medical care for the majority of those injured in the voting rights demonstrations One wonders what would have happened to the injured without this hospital...(March 26, 1965)

As the fallout of the events of "Bloody Sunday" was broadcast around the world, certainly Good Samaritan Hospital, hitherto unknown to the general population, now was a landmark of the struggle for civil rights. When the Sisters from around the country who had marched met with the Sisters of St. Joseph, they remarked that, although the press had focused on the oddity of Catholic nuns in the marches, "you Sisters have been giving witness down here for 30, almost 40 years." (Hite, 2002,p. 344). One of the most poignant results of that Sunday was the lasting friendship of John Lewis. Lewis was the head of the Student Non-Violent Coordinating Committee (SNCC) that organized and led the march of March 7, 1965. He arrived at Good Samaritan Hospital that day with several contusions and head trauma. In 2016, he visited the Motherhouse of the Sisters of St. Joseph in Rochester, and recounted his journey from being the son of a sharecropper in Troy, Alabama, to participating in the civil rights movement. Of his memories of "Bloody Sunday", he tearfully said: "Thank you for saving my life". (Video, Sisters of St. Joseph, October 26, 2016.

THE AFTERMATH

CERTAINLY for all those who witnessed this watershed event, the impressions, memories, and feelings about what became known as "Bloody Sunday" were indelible. But the Sisters had deeper mementos of that event. After all, Sisters of St. Joseph had been witness to this longer struggle for 35 years, years that people in the North had either not known about or chose to ignore. Theirs was the day- to -day accompaniment of the Black people to whom they ministered as they straddled worlds, white and black. They were the ones who tended to quotidian wounds, mental and physical, in almost total obscurity, for all those years. On "Bloody Sunday", though some of the Sisters were willing to ignore Archbishop Toolen's directive, it would seem that they gave truth to John Milton's words: "they also serve who only stand and wait".

In 2000, Sister Mary Paul Geck summed up the Selma experience:

Change was very gradual. Most of it was on the surface. Attitudes didn't change much, as far as white people were concerned. But change did come. Working in Selma was a tremendous expe-

rience. I feel glad and a little proud that we were part of chang-
ing history in Selma. It wasn't easy, to say the least, but we tried
our best to give witness of something as important as this. I'm glad
that we were there. It was definitely once in a lifetime. (The Bridge,
Summer, 2000)

It is important to note that the demonstration on March 7, 1965 was only one of three marches from Selma to Montgomery that took place. But the violence, shown and re-shown numerous times on national television, made it the galvanizing event of the effort. Martin Luther King, absent from the "Bloody Sunday" march, arrived later that same week and visited Good Samaritan Hospital. There an iconic photo showing Dr. King holding Etta Perkins' newborn daughter, was taken with Sisters Josepha Twomey, Bernice Quinn, Mary Weaver, Margaret Isabelle Tracy, and Mary Paul Geck. His presence drew multitudes from the North, including Jewish rabbis, Protestant ministers and Catholic priests. But most visible were Sisters in traditional habits from all over the United States, providing a very visible presence and a profound change in the perception of Catholic sisters in the country.

Perhaps it is the struggle witnessed by the Sisters, their participation in it, and a renewed sense of mission, hastened by the conclusion of the Second Vatican Council in 1965,that determined the fate of the Selma mission from the perspective of the Sisters of St. Joseph.

Vatican II, as it became known, was the brainchild of Pope John XXIII. He was concerned that the Church was an anachronism in a changing world, and was becoming irrelevant to the current generation of young people. The motto of the Council was *"aggiornamento"*-"update, modernize, speak to the present day, not to the past." Coincidentally, the year 1965 was a watershed year in many ways. That year saw the largest enrollment in Catholic schools: 6.5 million in 13,000 Catholic schools, (in 2020 that number was 1.2 million in 6,183 schools) and the largest number of women religious in the US: 181,000 (CARA, 2014). By 2018, there were 47,000.

Traditionally, Sisters were under the supervision of Bishops, priests, and congregational and local superiors. They worked in institutions, such as schools and hospitals. All the while, their community life was semi-cloistered: they lived in a convent, kept a specific horarium (schedule) of prayer and worship, and lived with the women with whom they worked all day. Their habit designated their state of life, and the particular religious order to which they belonged. They were to be, in the words of Thomas A'Kempis " in the world but not of it". Sister Margaret Traxler cites Cardinal Suenens, a "bright light" of the Council. She noted that the Cardinal pointed out:

> *Canon law looks upon [women religious] as minors and defines their conduct as though they were Victorian ladies destined only for Victorian drawing rooms. (Traxler, 1965, pp. 16-17).*

While the Second Vatican Council exhorted all religious orders-men and women- to go back to their roots and discover their true charism, and how they could relate to the world, it was the women religious who took this most seriously. For American Sisters, the very visible presence of Sisters in the marches subsequent to "Bloody Sunday" changed Sisters' lives in a profound manner. And that included the Sisters of St. Joseph. In fact, if one looks at the actions of the Sisters even from their arrival in 1940, they were certainly ahead of their time.

One change that was certainly most visible, was to the Sisters' habits. While the first Sisters had arrived in black serge habits and worked in the intense heat of Alabama summers, eventually, they were given permission to wear the same habit, designated as the "mission habit" only in white material that "breathed" and was more suited to the tropical climate. On January 25, 1967, Sister Vincentine noted in the annals: "The sisters wore the Mission Habit for the first time at the 5 PM Mass." Eventually, by the late 1960's, the Sisters were able to wear a habit much more suited to the climate of the South. It consisted of a gray skirt, white blouse, and a gray veil. Ironically, the Sisters, who had been considered "Black" by both Black and white Selmians, were now visibly straddling both communities in gray.

In January, 1967, the annals note that the Sisters had received and implemented permission for a more relaxed habit, consisting of a gray skirt, white blouse and "simple" headdress (designed by the famous Bergdorg Goodman of New York City). The Sisters no doubt anticipated some fascination with their "new look" on the day they wore it for the first time in school. However, on January 26, 1967, the school was broken into and vandalized, and the children had to stay outside while the police investigated. One student's observation swept away any excitement on the part of the students: "They may look different, but when they begin to teach, you know they are just the same."

As has been described above, the eventual product of integration was the demise of St. Elizabeth's School and, eventually, in 1976, the integrated Queen of Peace School. Concomitant to this was the loss of St. Elizabeth's parish, the parish of the Black Catholics. The demise of Good Samaritan Hospital followed the same trajectory.

By 1966, the hospital had undergone another expansion: a maternity ward, a pediatrics unit and 41-bed medical-surgical unit, three new operating rooms, a recovery room, and air conditioning. Along with the physical upgrades, the hospital introduced new therapies and equipment for cardiac patients. When the Medicare and Medicaid legislation was passed, the hospital's administrator, Sister Michael Ann, immediately worked to have the hospital certified to accept patients covered by these programs. It was a way to try to recoup the years of deficits that the hospital had carried with its load of indigent patients.

But this Medicare/Medicaid legislation forbade any discrimination in any facility that was reimbursed by Medicare and Medicaid. Very soon, the white doctors and their Black patients were seeking treatment and care in newer, more modern, and newly integrated hospitals which also accepted Medicare and Medicaid. Like the schools, hospitals such as Good Samaritan were the victims of their own success in the struggle for equal rights. After twenty years in existence, the Good Samaritan School of Practical Nursing closed in 1970. Nearby facilities were offering this training and Good Samaritan couldn't compete. Citing the need for Sister nurses in St. Joseph Hospital, and its own nursing school in Elmira, NY, which the Sisters of St. Joseph owned, the following year, 1971, the Sisters of St. Joseph officially withdrew from Good Samaritan Hospital. Note that this was the year that St. Elizabeth's School and Assumption School had merged to become Queen of Peace, leading, eventually, to that school's closure five years later.

The withdrawal from staffing the hospital did not end the Sisters' relationship with Good Samaritan. In July, 1978, the hospital received a grant of $160,000 for the operation of outreach clinics in three adjacent counties. Sisters Mary Weaver and Sister Jane Kelley, CSJ, a nurse practitioner from St. Louis, Missouri, were employed by this program and supported by the grant monies.

The hospital closed in 1983 with a debt of over $2 million (*Selma Times Journal, July 1, 1984*). The article noted:

> *The hospital provided care for many of the city's poor persons, and the large number of charity cases caused much of the financial problems which forced the closing.*

When the Sisters of St. Joseph left, the Daughters of Charity, who also ran a Catholic hospital in Mobile, took over the operation of Good Samaritan, and Sister Jane Kelly came too, but John Crear, who had become the hospital's first lay and first Black administrator noted, in 1983: "It was integration that killed Good Sam". (*Fitts, 2016, p. 284.*)

In 1984, two physicians, brothers, purchased the hospital from the Edmundite Fathers for $75,000. Their goal was to operate physicians' offices out of the former nursing home, but even this proved unsuccessful, and they abandoned the effort after two years. A visitor to Selma can view the hospital, abandoned, windows broken, showing marks of past fires, and derelict.

In 2016, a committee of Black citizens of Selma sought to reopen "Good Sam", not as a hospital, but as an out-patient clinic. The building was, at that time, owned by the Alabama Department on Economic and Consumer Affairs (ADECA). Lillie Smith, who headed the effort, commented:

> *I think it would be a good place to go, especially those who do not have the money (Selma Times Journal, July 25, 2016).*

Mayor George Evans noted that same year, that it would cost about $5 million just to make the building habitable again, and that the city of Selma would not put any funds into the effort. It would be up to the committee to raise the substantial funds to rehabilitate the building and secure a group to own and operate it. As of this writing (2021) that has not happened.

One final note: Sister Elizabeth Ann LeValley, who was President of the Sisters of St. Joseph from 1984 to 1992, recounts the story of Father Roger LaCharite, superior of the Society of St. Edmund. During a visit to Selma in 1988, Father approached Sister Elizabeth Ann with a request that the Sisters might house retired Edmundites at their motherhouse in Rochester, and Sister Elizabeth Ann thought it a splendid idea. For whatever reason, this did not come to pass, but Father LaCharite was so impressed that he offered to send to Rochester the stained glass window of Jesus with Black people that had been in the chapel of Good Samaritan Hospital. The "Good Samaritan" window arrived in 1988 and was installed at the Sisters' infirmary in 1990. When the new Motherhouse was completed in 2004, the window was moved and installed in a prominent place where anyone who enters that building cannot fail to notice it.

The Sisters recognized that buildings and institutions are only collateral tools for their work. Having shed the school and the hospital, the Sisters created a whole new set of ministries for the old challenges.

OLD CHALLENGES, NEW SOLUTIONS

WHILE THE HISTORIC FOCUS of the Sisters' work had been in the city of Selma, they realized that an even greater need existed in the more rural areas. Isolated from the many services available in the city, rural residents had no local facilities for health care or nutrition, and no means of transportation to reach those services. Furthermore, children's education took place in makeshift schools, and they lacked support and follow-up during summer recess.

Sister Mary Maloy arrived in Selma in 1982 at the age of 56. She had taught Latin, English, and Religion in the two high schools owned and operated by the Sisters in Rochester. After teaching, she became a guidance counselor in both of those schools, and this was wonderful preparation for what she was to do in Alabama, especially her gift for seeing what people needed. In a talk given to the parishes in Orville and Camden, AL, Sister Mary explained the shift in focus and the locus of the Sisters:

Some of you may be surprised that sisters are doing the works I've described (outreach activities). Perhaps you've known sisters only in the Catholic schools and Catholic hospitals, as was traditional in the U.S. in the early 20th century. That was the need at that time. You've heard me mention Sisters of St. Joseph several times and I want to use our history and tradition to explain this point. ...Sisters, at the very beginning were open to undertake any work which their times demanded...The first work of the sisters in the New World was teaching the deaf...The types of ministries are wide and varied, from the traditional teacher and hospital nurse to the more unusual...(Talk given November 3, 1985)

Bloody Sunday and its aftermath attracted several Sisters from many religious congregations, having recognized that the "home missions" were as needy as foreign postings. In fact, In fact, a total of 38 Sisters from a variety of Congregations and all parts of the country spent some time in the Selma area. As Carol Coburn notes:

> *After Selma, Sisters would never be found on the sidelines of social justice activism again. They moved center stage. Combined with the end of Vatican II and the cultural tensions, challenges and transitions of the 1960's, Selma thrust sisters into a new world spiritually, theologically, and socially. Selma signaled the beginning of what were often painful, but necessary and powerful transformations (Coburn, 2020)*

Hence, Sisters of Mercy, Sisters of St. Joseph of Carondolet, and Chambery, Daughters of the Holy Spirit, Sisters of Providence, Sisters for Christian Community, and Daughters of Charity who took over the staffing of the hospital, found their way into Selma to share community, charism, and mission. Sister Joan Marshall recalls:

> *Those were exciting days. We had so many Sisters from other communities, and we got along just fine. We expanded the convent to the house next door and a connector was built so that you could go from one house to the other without having to go outside. (Interview with Sister Joan Marshall, November 25, 2020).*

In their annual report to the Motherhouse in Rochester in 1975, the Sisters described their living arrangement:

> *The combined convent arrangement is a happy one. House government and duties are shared. Also shared are religious exercises of the Sisters, and recreational activities. The three communities form one convent family enjoying a special mission spirit of unity. (SSJ Archives)*

Carol Coburn, in the *Global Sisters Report* of March 9, 2015 noted:

> *After Selma and over the next 50 years, many Catholic sisters moved away from their historic contributions of creating and staffing educational, healthcare and social service institutions and gravitated to a variety of social justice issues and activities. Individuals, their religious communities, and the creation of many intercommunity networks and organizations helped reshape and redefine the response to social justice in late 20th-century America. (Global Sisters Report, National Catholic Reporter, March 9, 2015, p.1).*

Oddly, in 1975, 160 years after the arrival of the Sisters of Mercy, and 35 years after the Rochester Sisters arrived, and with the Queen of Peace Convent housing several Sisters of St. Joseph and a variety of Sisters from other communities, the Selma newspaper seems to have newly discovered that there were religious women in their midst. In an October 5, 1975 article in the Selma *Times Journal*, reporter Jane Jouret visited the convent at Queen of Peace and reported on what she considered a rather quaint phenomenon:

> *Dressed in garments that included contemporary-styled solid and gray patterned skirts worn with while blouses...a half-dozen of the sisters gathered in the convent's cheerful living room to talk about their life and work in Selma. Each sister has her own room in the spacious 100-year-old building...Decorated to suit the individual's taste, each room is kept spotlessly clean as is the entire convent.*

The question of what was next in terms of ministry was thoroughly discussed throughout the months of January and February of 1979:

> *On January 13, the Sisters met to discuss possibilities of new apostolates for Sisters in the future.*
>
> *January 24: Sisters met with Father Paul Morin and Father Richard Myhalyk, Regional Superior of the Edmundite Southern Mission to discuss new apostolates for the Sisters. No decisions were made.*
>
> *February 2: Father Morin: 'No new Edmundite funded apostolates for at least another year, but Sisters could apply for positions at Good Samaritan Hospital or in government funded programs'. (Annals for 1978-1979).*

With their usual inventiveness, the Sisters found something to do.

A 1978 Sisters of St. Joseph Newsletter article compiled by the Sisters in Alabama described the new focus:

> *Our work has gradually taken new directions. This was happening even before the discontinuance of our Sisters' presence at Good Samaritan Hospital and the closing of the school. New forms of service were evolving, and now that our work is no longer 'institution-based', we are branching out even more.*

The article went on to describe the new consensus-based governance of the parish, new religious education programs, standardization of home visits, tending to the spiritual needs of the sick, shut-ins, and the elderly, and providing direct assistance to the needy. The work of Sister Maureen Finn and Sister Albertine Devereaux in Queen of Peace Parish was also outlined. The article concluded, as always with:

There is much to be done, and we dream of the day when we shall have the presence and service of additional Sister in this small area of the South called the 'Selma Mission.'

In 1979, good Samaritan Hospital had established the Rural Health Initiatives program. The program established health clinics in Uniontown, Pine Apple and Yellow Bluff, all rural communities within a short drive from Selma. With the closure of the hospital in 1983, the clinics took on a major role in continued service to the poor in the Selma area. It also brought Sisters interested in direct aid to Selma to serve in the mission.

After the closure of the school, Sister Josette Capozzi, and then Sister Shirley Casler took on responsibilities at St. Joseph parish in Camden, Alabama, Sister Shirley partnered with an Edmundite priest to visit the elderly and sick in these small towns that had no services to determine people's needs. Sister Shirley also worked with the local Mennonites, who had begun a clinic several years before. In nearby Boykin,

Sister Josette, during that time, was, along with Sisters Grace Noel Gleichauf, and Marie Warth , involved in a serious auto accident in Mobile in 1980. After a total of twelve hours in surgery, Sister Joseette was on the way to recovery. Although the other Sisters were also injured, none was more serious than Sister Josette.

This was the second time Sisters had been injured in an auto accident; Sister Louis Bertrand had been seriously injured in 1963. In 2005, Sister Anita Kurowski, who was visiting Selma prior to her becoming a Sister, was injured, and, in 2020, Sister Nancy Clark was involved in a car accident that resulted in serious injury.

Sister Catherine Martin (Sister Catherine Theresa), who initially (1970) was the correspondence secretary and assistant editor of the Edmundite newsletter, also helped out at the Freedom Quilting Bee, an effort to encourage cottage industry among the rural women. She became so involved in the sewing cooperative, that she ceded her secretarial responsibilities to a Black woman whom she trained.

The production of beautiful, hand-made quilts was so impressive, that the United States Postal Service issued a series of full-color postage stamps in 2006. The famous quilts of Gee's Bend were thus marketed on every letter and card that bore the stamps, and the quilts were eventually acquired and sold by Lord and Taylor, an upscale national department store chain.

The Selma Sisters reported in a 1978 newsletter article to the Sisters in Rochester:

> There is no doubt that in Selma we have a vibrant and productive apostolate. Good things are going on. However, around us we see many material needs still not being met, and areas without a religious presence. There is much to be done, and we dream of the day when we shall have the presence and service of additional Sisters in this small area of the South called the "Selma Mission".

On the twentieth anniversary of "Bloody Sunday", people from Selma reflected on the aftermath and the changes that that event had wrought. Rev. Joseph Lowery, president of the Southern Christian Leadership Council, in 1985 noted: "Everything has changed and nothing has changed". (*America*, May 25, 1985, p.423).

What had changed was the commemoration of the event itself. Mayor Joe Smitherman, who had been Selma's mayor in 1965 and a bitter opponent of the march, was on hand, twenty years later, to welcome Black officials and church leaders, and to proclaim to them that Selma's integration efforts over the past two decades had been successful. But Sister Nancy Clark, who attended the event, noted: "Joe Smitherman sat in a cherry picker above the crowd. He couldn't bear to be in the midst of all these Black people." (Interview with Sister Nancy Clark, March 7, 2021). Selma's Black Catholics recounted how painful it had been to give up their parish and school, as St. Elizabeth's had become Queen of Peace, and their beloved church and school had closed. One of those parishioners observed, "now we all go to the same church together as brothers and sisters to worship God". (*America, May 25, 1985, p. 423*).

But many lamented the fact that, though they had gained political power, the Black community had not secured economic power. "What good does it do to control the county governments of Lowndes and Wilcox (counties) when they're among the poorest in the US?" (Ibid.) That same year (1985) the federal courts ruled that Selma's schools were fully integrated.(Fitts, 2016, p.306). The struggle among the Black community for political clout centered on the Selma public schools. Who would be the superintendent, who would be the school principals, and, even more important, who would constitute the Selma Public School Board were the issues that filled the 1970's and 1980's in Selma. Contentious meetings among the white mayor, Smitherman (yes, he of "Bloody Sunday"), and various groups of Black activists, the city council, and the school board often ended in frustrated upheaval.

What is known, however, is that the white population of Selma declined sharply during the 1980's, when white students made up 40% of the schools' enrollment. By 1985, white students made up only 30% of the public school enrollment, even though the courts had decreed that full integration had been achieved, and by 2005, Blacks made up 95% of the public school population. (Fits, 2016, p. 309)

White families had fled to other major cities, or to the suburbs, and, when Craig Air Force Base closed in 1977, white families from outside of Selma who had been assigned to the base, and who had supported integration, left the area. Notably, the only white children who attended the integrated Queen of Peace School were children of Air Force personnel assigned to Craig.

Bereft of the institutions that had provided the base for educational and health care ministries, the Sisters, as they had over the previous decades, adapted and prepared themselves for the next chapter in what was now called the "Alabama missions" due to the fact that the work had expanded beyond Selma into the heretofore neglected rural areas of central Alabama.

As has been cited above, in 1979, two years before its closing, Good Samaritan Hospital had established a Rural Health Initiative Program in Wilcox County by opening a clinic in Pine Apple, some 46 miles from Selma. At that time, the US Census reported that Pine Apple had 165 residents (the 2010 report lists 132); however, that figure is a "best guess" since the return on census forms was spotty at best.

In 1981, after Sisters of St. Joseph from other localities in the US had operated the clinic, Sister Mary Weaver became involved by offering to transport patients to Uniontown, in Perry County, for dental care, since the Pine Apple Clinic had no dentist nor did it have a dental hygienist. That ministry expanded to include her transporting patients to other hospitals and medical specialists. Sister Mary eventually became an employee of the county and coordinated government programs and grant monies for the rural assistance programs. The next year, 1982, Sister Mary Maloy began transporting patients in Pine Apple to clinic appointments, even though she resided in Selma.

While the focus on health was important, the Sisters also realized that the education that Black children were receiving was still not sufficient. Moreover, they found a dearth of literacy in the adults, and a lack of early childhood education. In August, 1985, Sister Nancy Clark arrived in Pine Apple and started a learning center to provide all-around education that included a pre-school, a remedial program for school-aged children, and adult education program, and a vacation school. In 1990, Sister Dorothy Quinn joined Sister Nancy, and, when Sister Dorothy was asked to return to Rochester, Sister Lorraine Julien, who had taught grades one and two in St. Elizabeth's School, replaced her, and stayed for the next ten years as Sister Nancy's assistant, even acting as director when Sister Nancy went on a sabbatical in 1995. As a sign of their commitment to this rural mission, the Sisters who worked in the learning center also lived in Pine Apple.

The Sisters lived in a neat white bungalow on the outskirts of Pine Apple, and commuted to their various ministries. Sister Patricia Flass recounts:

> Oh, we loved that house. It was so full of Sisters in the summer when Sisters came down from Rochester to volunteer in the summer school program. Sisters Kathy Fletcher, Anne Maura Morris, Rita Quigley, Carol Klem, Catherine Gibbons, and Concepta Vay were there various summers, and, after work, we'd go for picnics and other excursions in the area. (Interview with Sister Patricia Flass, February, 2021)

As had happened with St. Elizabeth School, Sisters volunteered their summers to come to Pine Apple to help out. What the children did not get in their public school, and what they were not receiving in their local community, the Sisters provided, from remediation to meals to recreational activities to outside experiences.

Sister Lorraine vividly remembers taking the children to a swimming pool:

> We went to the Brown YMCA. They loved the water, and even though they couldn't swim, they really enjoyed themselves. They took swim lessons; I was right in the pool with them and I can't forget the joy on their faces". (Interview with Sister Lorraine Julien, November 25, 2020).

Sister Catherine Gibbons, a veteran educator who had taught in inner-city Rochester, as well as more rural areas in the twelve-county Diocese of Rochester, fondly remembers her summer in Pine Apple in 1995:

> I had taught in an inner-city Catholic school (St. Bridget's) and I have to say that the children in our program in Pine Apple were much more receptive to the offerings we had available. Their lives revolved around multi-generational living situations. We picked them up each morning and then drove them home every afternoon when the summer school finished. Those at the "end of the line", the last ones dropped off, told stories of their grandparents and scores of aunts and uncles that impacted their day to day lives. They had so little, so that, any time we offered an experience or even the chance to see friends in a classroom setting, they loved it. I have to say that my time with them in the classroom teaching problem solving skills and math were the best time of the day." (Interview with Sister Catherine Gibbons, January 31, 2021)

ENCULTURATION AND AN EDUCATION IN SOCIAL JUSTICE

THE Sisters realized that, in rapidly changing times, they needed to educate themselves in the issues, efforts, and history being tackled by the Black people of the South. And so, in addition to the work that they did during the week, "down time" was occupied by their attendance at conferences, classes, and seminars. In 1986, they began attending the annual Catholic Committee of the South, networking with others, who, like themselves, had dedicated their energies to improving the lot of Black people in the

South. Sisters Nancy Clark and Anne Urquhart took extension classes in Black theology from Xavier University. In 1987, the Sisters of St. Joseph in Pine Apple hosted and sponsored a leadership workshop in conjunction with Tuskegee University to train local people for community leadership positions within their communities. Finally, Sisters Mary Weaver and Nancy Clark committed one weekend each month, starting in 1987, to attending a course in Black culture from Xavier University in Birmingham. From the arrival of the Sisters in 1940, where they were accepted by the Black community in Selma, the Sisters forty years later took positive steps to deepening their understanding of that acceptance.

NEW MODELS OF MISSION: SELMA

SISTER Maureen Finn continued to use the facilities of St. Elizabeth's mission to do social outreach to the Black community. In fact, under her leadership, Queen of Peace Parish became the first parish in the Archdiocese of Mobile to set up a parish-based social ministry. The program included the still-observed tradition of providing hot meals to shut-ins on Thanksgiving Day when all the other social service agencies were closed. Sister Maureen provided assistance to families in securing government services, counseled adults in crisis, and gave small amounts of money to people who were unable to meet obligations such as utilities and meals, while the parish established a program that, today (2021) provides several hundred meals every day of the year. Sister Marilyn Pray recalls substituting for Sister Maureen while Sister Maureen visited family in Rochester: "*She left me with $100. What was I going to do with $100? They just kept coming and coming and asking for help, and all I had was $100!*" Obviously the need for hands-on help was daunting.

When a nutrition program was begun in 1978, Sister Maureen felt that she did not have time to attend to it. She hired Tommie Byrd, who had been the substitute teacher at St. Elizabeth's School and eventually Queen of Peace School, to run that program.

By 1978, Sisters Albertine Devereaux and Maureen Finn were on a parish team that included the Edmundite Fathers that updated the parish lists and made home visiting more routinized. The Sisters organized weekly Mass in one of the three nursing homes in Selma, and made visits to the sick and elderly a priority.

Sister Mary Weaver, by 1978, was employed in a government-financed project, Neighborhood Services, a division of the Community Action Program, a grass-roots organization whose goal was to give assistance to the needy and elderly of the area. Sister Mary came to Selma in 1974, at the age of 40, and, with the exception of two years in Rochester to recover from health problems, spent eighteen years in Selma and the Selma area.

As Assistant Executive Director of the Dallas County Action Agency, she oversaw a daycare program, a housing repair program, an energy assistance program, and a food distribution program. She recounts, in an October 20, 1989 summary of her work:

> I met Bessie in 1970, when Community Action was setting up a senior citizen center. I went around areas of the city, urging the elderly to come to the center. On a certain day I found Bessie with a raft of children. Her husband had left her after she had had a stroke. She was living in a horrible home, but she truly wanted to better her condition.
>
> I was able to vouch for her loan so that she could buy a trailer. A man from our parish helped with her plumbing and heating. When her daughter, who had two children, was widowed, Bessie took in these children. Today, the children help Bessie financially, and this assistance, together with a certain amount of social security gives Bessie a measure of comfort and security.
>
> Bessie stays in touch. She calls me early in the morning, sometimes just to chat.

It is obvious that Sister Mary Weaver had adopted the people of Selma as much as they had adopted her. Her many years in Selma, spent with the shy, painfully introverted personality with which she was blessed, spoke eloquently of her devotion to the people of Alabama.

At this time, some of the Sisters were concerned that their lives in Selma did not reflect the abject poverty that they saw in the area. The archives for the convent in 1978 report:

> The first of five weekly meetings in which the subject of religious poverty was studied, as planned during (Superior General of the Sisters of St. Joseph) Sister Jamesine's (Riley) visit in February. Sister Maureen and Sister Shirley expressed a desire to live a radical life of poverty.

Eventually, as will be described, three of the Sisters moved to another house in the Black neighborhood.

House meeting minutes clearly illustrate the struggle the Sisters dealt with to live what they preached, and to maintain a healthy spiritual life as well as a well-rounded community routine. The Sisters spent three days-October 4, 6,and 7 in 1976 coming to terms in what qualities they wanted in a local coordinator (previously superior) in the convent. A summary of these qualities is listed in their final document:

> *The coordinator for the SSJ community in Selma through the power of the Spirit and community support strives to be: one who draws forth in loving concern the best in each member...one who observes with loving kindliness the principles of religious government...one who communicates with the SSJ congregation...and strives to strengthen the group in areas of accountability, sharing, co-responsibility, decision making. (Minutes of Queen of Peace Convent, October,1976).*

Clearly the Sisters of the 1970's met the challenge of imagining their lives in light of the Second Vatican Council, their experience in the South, and their coping with the distance between where they lived and the Motherhouse in Rochester.

With respect to ministry, what was different from the original efforts of the Sisters in Selma in the 1940's was the fact that the Sisters of the 1970's and 1980's realized that their efforts would be stymied unless they formed partnerships. Reflecting the community life that they led that included Sisters from other congregations, they reached out to organizations outside the Catholic sphere. Health education programs sponsored by the University of Alabama at Birmingham, and Auburn University, a Black Women's Group, parenting classes for young mothers and Family Life programs at Jones High School were visible efforts at partnerships with public and private groups.

Sisters began attending the Catholic Committee of the South annually and contacted Arnett Lewis, director of the Rural Organizing and Cultural Center (ROCC) in Mississippi. Using the ROCC model, Sisters Mary Maloy and Nancy Clark organized vocal demand for clean water in the rural areas and forced Wilcox County to make sure that residents had clean drinking water. The new working model for the Sisters was the involvement of the people themselves in the demand for basic services from local government. This empowerment of the residents enabled the Sisters to look to new ministries and areas in need of attention.

Further collaboration with Wilcox County resulted in Sister Remigia McHenry's being hired by the county to visit the elderly sick, train home health care aides, and enable residents to access health care. In 1988, a coalition of religious and other grassroots organizations created Alabama Arise, and Sister Anne Urquhart was one of the original members. Eventually all Sisters of St. Joseph in the Selma area became part of this organization, with Sister Mary Maloy becoming a member of its board of directors in 1997. The mission of Alabama Arise was the involvement of local people in the changes to public policy so that the needs of low income residents would not be neglected. Sister Mary Maloy attended the Alabama Arise Retreat in Columbiana, Alabama to celebrate the tenth anniversary of the founding of the organization in August, 1998.

Although the Edmundite Fathers had, from the outset, secured funds to support their ministries, it is important to note that students from both Nazareth College and Nazareth Academy regularly sent money, clothing, schoolbooks, and other supplies to the Sisters. Later on, students from Nazareth Academy, and Aquinas Institute, another Catholic high school in Rochester, New York, would travel to Selma during their Easter vacation to volunteer in the various ministries. The Society for the Propagation of the Faith in Rochester had an annual appeal and raised considerable funds for the Selma mission due to the fact that the Sisters provided a "Selma connection" with Rochester. In a May 7, 1975 issue of the Catholic diocesan newspaper, the *Catholic Courier-Journal*, Father Joseph Reinhart, director of the diocesan missions office remarked:

> *For 35 years the diocese has been giving witness in Selma, Alabama through our Sisters of St. Joseph. Their presence in Selma has done much to bring the love and concern of Christ to the people they have met and worked with. So when diocesans contribute to the Missions appeal, they can be assured that the assistance will be transformed into Christian work where it is needed...*

And last, but certainly not least, the Congregation of the Sisters of St. Joseph of Rochester provided considerable resources, the most important of which were Sisters, to this effort. Were it not for the interest of Mother

Rose Miriam in aiding the Black people of the South, and her prodigality in supporting what she had committed to, the plight of the Black people of Selma might never had had the experience of white Catholics adopting their causes. Edmundite Father Lambert, in a paean to Mother Rose Miriam, lauded her efforts:

> Your missionary spirit overflowed into the Deep South and your Sisters came to Alabama. The work in Selma has enjoyed great success and it is due in great part to the zeal, prayers, and sacrifices of the Sisters of St. Joseph. All the Edmundites join with me in expressing a simple by most sincere 'thank you and God bless you, Mother (Letter of Father Lambert to Mother Rose Miriam, August 31, 1951).

But in the spirit of collaboration, the now so-called "Alabama Mission" was able to obtain other funding. The partnerships with federal, state, and local agencies gave the Sisters access to monetary and other resources. Civil rights legislation unleashed a torrent of federal monies, including Medicare and Medicaid, and massive funding for education. Several grants were secured for specific projects, and the grantors thus established partnerships and collaborative efforts with the Sisters. The solidity of the new ministries and the transparency of the use of resources won new-found admiration for the Sisters.

PINE APPLE

SEVERAL PROJECTS AROSE IN this little settlement forty-six miles from the city of Selma that closely mirrored the original efforts of the 1940's. While the original Sisters undertook visiting the sick and shut-ins, catechizing adults and children, starting and operating a school, and establishing the hospital and nursing school, the Sisters realized that the sphere of these ministries needed to be provided, but in a different way.

Thus, as has been noted above, Sister Nancy Clark established a learning center in 1985. This was the formalization of a summer education program that had been started in 1984 by Sister Mary Maloy. While the children attended the local public school during the day, the Sisters conducted an adult education program at that time. They worked to eradicate the widespread adult illiteracy, helped people to secure their high school diplomas, and in so doing, offered a community atmosphere for people who otherwise were isolated in this rural area. Eventually, a Toddlers and Moms program was begun that further socialized adults, and taught them good parenting skills, and healthy living information.

Sister Nancy Clark explained the establishment of the learning center:

> When I arrived in Selma in 1985, the Edmundites gave me $2,000 and a van and told me to go to Pine Apple and see what needed to be done. Sister Jane Kelley, who worked in the health clinic, told me that the children couldn't read. So, I went over to the public school, and volunteered to teach computers to the kids. I figured that no one would have a problem with that. When I met with the principal, a white man, he told me, 'You know, most of these kids are bastards' (sic). So I saw with my own eyes that the children were being short-changed in their education. (Interview with Sister Nancy Clark, March 7, 2021).

Sister Nancy spent the next 27 years in Pine Apple thoughtfully expanding the offerings of the learning center.

There was a Head Start program that only had limited resources, and could not accommodate all of the three- and four-year-olds. So Sisters Nancy Clark and Lorraine Julien, who came to help Sister Nancy in 1990, headed out in their van each day to pick up the youngest children, in order to provide for them what Head Start, a federally funded program, could not. After school, the children were provided remedial education and enrichment, thus filling in the gaps left by the notably inadequate educational program provided by the public school. Sister Marie Albert Alderman, who served in Alabama, reported:

[Sisters] Nancy and Lorraine maintain an excellent working relationship with the principal and teachers of the [public] elementary school and are welcomed by the students. The two sisters volunteer their services there weekly. (Interview with Sister Marie Albert Alderman, January 14, 1994)

In order that the children not fall behind in the summer months, vacation school, which provided recreation, remediation, and enrichment with arts and crafts, music, dance, and physical education were offered. Many Sisters came from Rochester to volunteer their time. Sister Concepta Vay spent 16 summers in Pine Apple. She taught Bible classes and worked with the youngest children. *"We started out with a four-week program, but it filled up so fast that we couldn't accommodate all the children who wanted to attend, so we had two two-week programs in order to take more kids". (Sister Nancy Clark, March 7, 2021)*

Even more notable, the sisters working in Pine Apple moved out of the convent on Broad Street in Selma to a small house, which they named St. Joseph's Convent. The new little community consisted of Sister Kathleen Stack, CSJ, from St. Louis, Missouri, and who had served for 23 years in Japan, and Sister Mary Maloy. By July, 1998, three Sisters of St. Joseph, Sister Mary Maloy, Sister Lorrain Julien, and Sister Nancy Clark would inhabit the little white house in Pine Apple. And by January, 1999, Sister Kathleen Navarra and Sister Patricia Flass would join them. Sister Mary wrote, in December , 1984 of the welcome they received.

The people have been very hospitable to us since we arrived on September 30. They seem genuinely happy to have us here. And we like being with them. A week ago Sister Kathleen and I attended a barbeque and this past Sunday we were invited to attend the Sunday service at the Macedonia Baptist Church. One of our clinic ladies, who is a missionary in the church, gave the sermon. (Report to the Congregation, December, 1984)

While, as noted above, the Sisters of St. Joseph were continually trying to entice more Sisters to the Alabama mission, the vacation school was an attractive alternative, due to the short duration of the work. Nonetheless, it is remarkable that Sisters who taught all year in the schools of the Diocese of Rochester, volunteered to perform this demanding work in a daunting milieu with children with so many needs. Sisters Concepta Vay, (who came down for 16 summers) Kathleen Fletcher, Carol Klem, Ann Maura Morris, Rita Quigley, Catherine Gibbons and many laypersons spent several summers in the Learning Center in Pine Apple.

The learning center, which had been directed by Sister Nancy Clark, closed in 2012. At that time, Sister Nancy, and Sister Janet Connorton, who had been working with Sister Nancy, moved back to Selma to live in an apartment. That same year, Sisters Patricia Flass and Kathleen Navarra (who had left the house in Pine Apple to live in a trailer in Vredenburgh) left Vredenburgh and moved to Selma, even though Sister Patricia continued her work in Pine Apple, and Sister Kathleen assumed the role of Educational Ministries in Selma, Mosses (another small settlement), and Vredenburgh. When Sisters Patricia and Kathleen returned to Selma, Sisters Nancy and Janet moved from their apartment to Queen of Peace Convent, originally the home of the Sisters of Mercy who taught at Assumption School. Thus the convent at 2511 Summerfield Road, which had served as the parish rectory after the departure of the Sisters of Mercy, supplanted the original house at 1423 Broad Street, that had welcomed the first Sisters 74 years earlier.

When the original Sisters arrived in Selma in 1940, they took over the operation of the so-called "Clothing Room", noting that clothes were the currency of the Black community. Sister Mary Maloy had begun a thrift shop in 1982. Notably, there was no retail location for the people of Pine Apple to shop. Father David Cray, an Edmundite priest, quipped: "Once a poor family that lived in this area paid for the gas to drive to Camden or Selma to shop, it didn't have the money left to buy the clothes it needed." (Pine Apple bulletin, June, 1995).

Sister Mary Maloy's vision of a thrift shop and luncheonette became reality in 1995 with the building of the Partners Shop, which offered donated clothes and snacks for sale at a reasonable price. Sister Mary noted:

> *This isn't just a dream come true. It's also a beautiful example of*
> *what the Missions is all about—helping people to help themselves.*
> *(Pine Apple Bulletin, June, 1995)*

The shop was so popular that many volunteers traveled from the North to Pine Apple, to work in the shop and help out with other tasks, but the Edmundites had nowhere to house them. In November, 1994, the Edmundites purchased a double wide trailer as a residence, and a parcel of land for the thrift store. A cement block structure was erected at a cost of $43,798.51, and serves as a senior center, an after-school learning center, and a tornado shelter.(Archives, *Pine Apple/Wilcox County*).

In June, 1995, when the Snack Bar and Thrift Shop was opened, the people of Pine Apple not only had a place to purchase necessities, but they had a place to socialize, network, and interact with the volunteers from the Northern United States. At the volunteer recognition dinner in 2000, the Snack Bar and Thrift Shop was re-named Mary's Food and Fashion in honor of Sister Mary Maloy who had created it and helped it to flourish. Pine Apple now had a clinic, a thrift shop, a snack bar, a senior center, and a learning center.

Together with the aforementioned Pine Apple Clinic, begun in 1979, the Learning Center, Thrift Shop, and Snack Bar loosely mirrored those first efforts of the 1940's. Moreover, the existence and growth of these efforts meant that volunteers from other parts of the country had several options for service in the now-called Alabama Mission. College and high school students donated their spring or winter or summer breaks to help with visiting and operating the various ministries. More important than the service they provided was the opportunity to do "reverse mission"; that is, carrying back to their homes the nature of the ministries and the huge need for help with them. Most of all, they conveyed the message that the passage of the civil rights legislation did not miraculously erase decades of poverty and depression and could not be lost in the euphoria that had permeated the country in the 1960's.

Father Roger LaCharitè, Superior of the Society of St. Edmund, was featured in an interview with the Jesuit publication, *America*. He observed:

> *We're now reaching more patients through our clinics than we used to reach through the hospital. And in another year we'll be reaching more students through our learning centers than we used to reach through our mission school. In Selma, 30% of the families live below the poverty line and that's heartbreaking. But look at the towns in Wilcox County. Pine Apple has 48% of its people below the line and Vredenburgh has 58%. That's where we have to concentrate our limited resources. (Father Roger La Charitè, America Magazine, May 25, 1985)*

THE KELLOGG GRANT AND POTABLE WATER

EVEN more pressing than the clothing and snack shop was the availability of potable water. Most of the homes in Pine Apple, particularly among the elderly, had no indoor plumbing. This meant that water had to be drawn daily from wells, and, as one resident, Annie Johnson explained, "Even when there is water in the well, it's unfit to drink." (Birmingham *Post-Herald*, October 17, 1988). Sisters Mary Maloy, Nancy Clark, and Kathleen Stack, a CSJ from St. Louis, urged the residents of Pine Apple to attend county commission meetings to push for water service

Eventually, these sisters established the Wilcox Rural Action Committee, a group representing nine county committees, since the water problem went beyond Pine Apple and Wilcox County.

When the committee contacted the Kellogg Foundation, representatives from the foundation were sent to assess the need. A press release from the Sisters of St. Joseph described what they saw:

> *Kellogg Foundation representatives were shocked at the conditions they found in Wilcox County, where they recently visited to investigate the need for a project to supply drinking water to the county's several hundred residents. When Sister Mary Maloy*

toured the Kellogg officials through the county's poorer areas, the officials compared Wilcox County to a third-world country...Sister Mary Maloy show[ed] the Kellogg representatives the homes of the elderly. 'My role was to take [the representatives] to their houses and then to ask, 'Is it the best thing to keep the elderly in this environment? Most of their homes are in need of tremendous structural repair...for the elderly to stay in their homes, they need water!' (SSJs of Rochester Strong Leaders in Fight for Water in Wilcox County, Alabama, June 24, 1988)

The result was that the committee received a grant of $300,000 from the Kellogg Foundation; though the project was to cost over $1 million, the state of Alabama agreed to cover the $800,000 shortfall. The Sisters of St. Joseph Newsletter of June 17, 1988 announced to the Rochester Congregation:

For the first time in eastern Wilcox County, Alabama, about 2000 elderly people will look forward to turning on a faucet for water instead of walking to the creek and carrying water home. Sisters Mary Maloy and Nancy Clark have been strong leaders in obtaining the grants for this vital water system, and all the complexities of legislatures, boards, groups with vested interests tested their mettle.

Thus one of the first attempts at political action involving the residents of this rural area bore fruit and spawned an interest in other projects. Both Sister Mary Maloy and Sister Nancy Clark were enthusiastic about expanding their efforts. They traveled to New Orleans on June 10 of 1988 to attend a forum on housing and, in an interview with the Birmingham *Post-Herald* the Sisters explained the motivation behind their ministry:

'We saw that water had to come first before housing', said Sister Mary. The new water expansion –construction expected to begin in the fall-won't reach the residents who need it around Pine Apple (that is, outside the town limits) but, quoting Sister Nancy and Sister Mary, 'It's a step closer!' The sisters already talk about further water line expansions. 'We'll find other ways, other possibilities,' maintained Sister Nancy. And Sister Mary concluded, 'We try to

do what we can, but mostly we try to be supportive, to be with the
people and respect them as they are.'

Sister Mary Maloy dug deeper into her presence among the people of the Deep South. She marveled at the generous receptivity that the people afforded her, a native of the North, an interloper, one trying to understand the very soul of the Black people of Alabama. In a rhapsodic reflection that she wrote, in 1990, she struggled with the "differentness" that she presented to a people who asked for so little, and lamented her lack of understanding:

I was swept up. That is, my spirit was swept up: my stiff disciplined white
body does not sway, claps awkwardly on the odd beat, holds itself primly in
check, never lets go. But I held the hands near me, gripping with all my might,
hoping that some electricity of praise and joyousness would connect somehow
on "We Shall Overcome", ashamed of my careful liturgies, my strangled pat-
terns of praying. Nowhere was I so aware of how little I had to give.

However little Sister Mary Maloy felt she understood, she was loved and revered by the people among whom she worked. When she died in 2008, her extensive obituary quoted Brown O'Quinn, a local Baptist minister, who called her "an instrument of God". The picture that accompanied her obituary showed Sister Mary with her dear Selma friends, Lula and Doris Smith.

Upon the death of Sister Mary Maloy, Doris Smith, who had worked with Sister Mary, took over the operation of Mary's Food and Fashion. At that time, Pine Apple hosted a learning and tutoring center, which included an early childhood center, a rural health clinic, a senior nutrition program, a food pantry, and the clothing and snack shop.

Sister Jane Kelley, CSJ, from St. Louis, who came to Selma in 1972 to work at Good Samaritan Hospital, was in on the beginning of the health clinic, which was also sponsored by the Edmundites, though it had been begun by Good Samaritan Hospital before the Sisters left that institution. She later persuaded Dr. Rosanne Cook, a physician and CSJ from St. Louis, to come in 1986 to Pine Apple, and Sister Theresa Kvale, CSJ, California, in 1980, to take her place while she pursued her nurse practitioner's license.

We saw mostly diabetes, hypertension, anemia, and pica- an
eating disorder in which the people ate the clay from the ground

and was very prevalent. We once went over to the store that sold white clay and tried to persuade the owner to stop selling the clay. I said 'you know this is wrong', and he pointed to a rather imposing man and said 'you tell him'. The man was imposing, and I didn't want to confront him. It's still being done to this day, and the local people still send it to family in Detroit. (Interview with Sister Jane Kelley, CSJ, February 16, 2021).

The nineteen nineties saw a veritable spate of social organizing, interdenominational, and partnering activities in Pine Apple done by the Sisters. The annals of the convent in Pine Apple, compiled by Sister Lorraine Julien, chronicle the activity for 1998-1999:

On September 26 (1998), Alabama Arise held its tenth anniversary celebration in Montgomery. It was attended by [Sisters] Mary (Maloy), Kathleen (Navarra), Lorraine (Julien), and several members of Partners in Progress.

On November 21 and 22]Sisters] Mary, Kathleen, and Lorraine together with Sister Marie Albert (Alderman) drove to Fort Benning, Georgia to participate in the weekend protest against the existence of the School of the Americas.

On November 27 and 28, Sisters Mary, Kathleen, and Lorraine attended the [C/SSJ] Federation South meeting held in Mississippi.

On December 1 and 2, Sister Lorraine attended the Governor's Conference in Birmingham on Parenting, a two-day conference for parents and professionals dealing with children.

On the ninth of January (1999), Sisters Mary, Nancy, and Lorraine attended the Alabama Arise annual goal-setting meeting in Montgomery.

On January 9, Sister Pat (Flass) and Sister Anne Urquhart traveled to New Orleans for the Hofinger Religious Education Congress.

In March, we attended the Bridge Crossing Jubilee in Selma to commemorate the Bloody Sunday crossing in 1965.

From April 10 to April 15 Sisters Pat and Kathleen attended the National Black Catholic Congress in Kentucky.

Sisters Nancy, Kathleen, and Mary attended a Housing Author-

ity meeting in Camden on April 21.

April 26 and 27, Sisters Mary and Kathleen attended the Lobby Day at the Capitol Building in Montgomery and the Legislative Reception following.

On June 15, Sister Kathleen attended a HUD/ADECA(Alabama Department of Economics and Commerce Agency) meeting in Montgomery to discuss tax reform. (Selected entries from 1998-1999 annals of St. Joseph Convent in Pine Apple).

It was clear to see that the Sisters were now closely engaged in networking with organizations that would not only educate them on systemic needs needing systemic remedies, but would provide for a sense of "presence" and witness of the Sisters of St. Joseph in the larger arena of their ministry.

In 2012 the Learning Center in Pine Apple closed and Sister Nancy Clark, who had begun the center, and Sister Janet Connorton, who had been working with Sister Nancy, moved to Selma. What precipitated the closing was the movement of all the elementary and high school students to schools in Camden, and, with a dearth of elementary students, the Edmundites withdrew their funding of the center, even though, by that time, Sister Nancy had a full complement of pre-kindergarten children. (Interview with Sister Nancy Clark, March 7, 2021) At that time, the senior center, which was attached to the learning center, also closed. The rural clinic was taken over by the county health department and operates to this day.

When Sister Nancy left Selma to return to Rochester in 2014, Sister Janet worked at the Senior Center at the Edmundite property in Selma until June, 2016. Sister Patricia Flass, who had moved to Vredenburgh in 2008 drove the hour's trip each day to Pine Apple to work as Director of Outreach and the Food Pantry. Although Sister Patricia moved to Selma in 2014, she continued to visit Pine Apple every day to conduct her ministries.

When one visits Pine Apple today, one can see that the former Learning Center is now a county-run rural health clinic, and Mary's Food and Fashion continues its services. It is directed and operated by a woman with whom Sister Mary Maloy had opened the facility, Doris Smith.

The store opened in 1995 and it was after a meeting with the community that Dr. Roseanne Cook did a presentation at the uni-

versity of Tuscaloosa. There was a man there by the name of Dr.
McQueen and he ran a volunteer program in Tuscaloosa. Sister
Mary Maloy was dealing with outreach and I worked with her. Af-
ter Dr. McQueen talked with Sister Mary, he explained that people
can improve their lives by having things for sale.

We began to get people to donate goods and we would sell them
for very little. We started selling on the sidewalk, and then we got
this building. Sister Mary would give people money for utilities
or food and, in exchange, they would give time to the thrift shop.
That's how Sister Mary got people to be invested in this shop. (In-
terview with Doris Smith, February 15, 2021).

Sister Kathleen Navarra, who arrived in Pine Apple in 1998, engineered
the addition of a laundry facility on one end of the Food and Fashion
building. Utilizing her expertise from the inception of the Building a Better
Community in Vredenburgh, another grass-roots effort, Partners in Progress, sprang up. Sister Kathleen explained:

Father Roger (La Charitc) said that we had no more money
to run the various ministries in Pine Apple, and that we needed
to leave. So we went to the people and asked them if they want-
ed to give up all that had been done. They refused and used their
own energy to carry on what we had started. (Interview with Sister
Kathleen Navarra, February 15, 2021)

But time has not been kind to Pine Apple. Families, especially young
people, have moved out of this little settlement, either to Northern cities to
look for work, or to more developed areas with more amenities. The little
white house that Sisters inhabited when they worked in the rural areas
around Selma has been sold to a private family. The Edmundite Congregation has moved out of Pine Apple, but Wilcox County has stepped up to
do what it should have done in the first place: look out for the needs of its
citizens. The County can never have the passion and the dedication that
the Sisters poured into their efforts, but as the population of the area has
diminished, and people have left, the lasting legacy of their caring ministrations lingers.

VREDENBURGH

IN ADDITION TO THE ministries in Pine Apple, the settlement of Vredenburgh received attention for its needs. Vredenburgh, about an hour south of Selma, according to the 2010 Census, harbored 312 residents; however, nine years later (2019) its population is 241 in a total area of 1.5 square miles. It is composed of 10.7% white, 88.9% Black, and .31% other races. The median income for a household in Vredenburgh is $27,321 and 27.7% of the population live below the poverty line, including 35.3% of people under the age of 18, and 30.4% of those over the age of 65. Almost 40% of the households have females with children and no male present. (Wikipedia, January 18, 2021). The major employer in the area was the Vredenburgh Saw Mill, owned by Peter Vredenburgh after whom the town was named.

When the sawmill was in operation, it ran like the storied "company towns" featured in the muckraking novels of the early twentieth century. The sawmill built and owned the houses inhabited by the employees, the general store and gas station, the park and the public works were all owned by the paper mill. There were separate facilities for the Black residents, and the mill provided employment, according to race, of course, and income to the town, even though workers' pay was in company dollars, worthless anywhere but the local company-owned stores. In 1962 the mill burned down, and, with it, the culture and the history that had created Vredenburgh in the first place, leaving the town bereft of most of its residents. The company deeded the houses to the people who stayed, but many of those houses are in grave disrepair at present. Residents have been able, through some government programs, to purchase house trailers, and these dot the lanes that mark what now constitutes the settlement of Vredenburgh.

For several years, Sister Shirley Casler, in partnership with Sister Rose-anne Cook, a CSJ from St. Louis and a medical doctor, directed the rural health center known as the Alberta Clinic, which had been started in 1978. Sister Marie Albert Alderman, in a January 14, 1994 report to the Sisters of St. Joseph, noted:

The Alberta Clinic has its share of challenges which Sister Shirley is addressing with her considerable experience, skill, and compassion.

Sister Shirley also was the pastoral assistant at two other Wilcox County towns: Orville and Camden. She was involved in almost all aspects of parish life in these towns, including the religious education program, planning the liturgies, home visits, parish census, and preparing the Catholics in those areas to receive the sacraments

That same year (1978), a health clinic was established in nearby Perry County. In preparation for serving the most needy, Sister Mary Weaver spent weeks visiting homes and acquainting the people with the nature of the health services that would be provided. She helped in the final preparations for the opening of the clinic and then served as its receptionist and secretary. In the meantime, she did daily hospital visits and did home care follow-up of patients.

When Sister Mary Weaver died that same year at the age of 70 in 2004, Father Roger LaCharitè noted:

Sister Mary was a remarkable minister. When adapted to the changes brought about by Vatican II becoming our first nun to join the staff of a secular organization in order to serve the poor. She served as Associate Pastor of Queen of Peace, she served as office manager for the Rural Health Initiative, and she also ran the Bosco Nutrition Center (at the Edmundite Mission House). (Selma Times-Journal, September 14, 2004)

In the meantime, Sister Patricia Flass had arrived in Vredenburgh in 2008 and lived in the trailer with Sister Kathleen Navarra, who had been there since 2004, Sister Marie Albert Alderman, and two Sisters of St. Joseph from Hartford, Connecticut. Although Sister Patricia's ministry was Director of Outreach and Food Pantry in Pine Apple, an hour away, she occasionally traveled to Selma to teach adult religious education.

Sister Kathleen Navarra, who trained in teaching and religious studies, transferred from the Sisters of St. Joseph of Watertown, New York to the Sisters in Rochester in 1989, and came to the Selma area in 1998. In 2008, after Sister Patricia Flass arrived, Sister Kathleen worked with local agencies to secure grants for local infrastructure projects such as road and sewer improvements. She also facilitated the creation of a town council, that continued to secure grants and other donations for a playground near a trailer where an after school learning program was held. (Archives, Sisters of St. Joseph of Rochester)

A community organizing and empowerment agency, Building a Better Community, was born out of the Edmundites' need to relinquish, in 2008, the ministries that the Sisters had begun because they were short of funds. This grassroots effort grew out of that withdrawal of the Edmundites, and Sister Kathleen began the agency with the belief that the local people, with a serious stake in their welfare, could solicit funds for the continuation of the work done by the Sisters.

With Building a Better Community, Sister Kathleen also coordinated the building of a sturdy structure that now sits next to the clothing cupboard, Wise Buys. The new building houses a senior day care, after-school tutoring for pre-teens and teens, and serves as a shelter from tornadoes and hurricanes. Wise Buys, which offers clothing and other household items at drastically reduced prices, moved from its former location next to the Vredenburgh Post Office in 2018.

Sisters Patricia and Kathleen also partnered with Prince of Peace Parish in nearby Hoover, Alabama, to provide Christmas gifts for children and the elderly and, together, the parishioners and Sister Kathleen secured a major grant to build the community center in Vredenburgh.

In 2014, the Learning Center in Pine Apple closed, but an after-school program and a summer program were moved to the new location of Wise Buys. High school and college students came to Vredenburgh, stayed in the trailer once occupied by the Sisters, and helped out with the summer education programs.

By 2017, Sister Kathleen Navarra also became the Director of the After School and Food Ministry Program in Mosses, Alabama. By that time, she and Sister Patricia had moved into the convent at Queen of Peace Parish in Selma, after the Edmundite Fathers, who had lived there for several years, moved into an apartment.

Mosses, Alabama is in Lowndes County, a part of the greater Montgomery metro area. The 2020 census reported that there are 1,020 residents there, and the median household income is $24,989. The poverty rate is 44.1%, making the area one of the poorest in Alabama (City-Data.com).

In December, 2021, the CBS program, *60 Minutes*, did a segment on the lack of sewage facilities in Lowndes County. They pointed out that the residents could not afford to install septic systems in their houses, and the county has not provided for sewer hookup with the county waste disposal system. Therefore, raw, untreated sewage continues, day after day, to leach into the soil and eventually into the waterways in the area, fouling the water sources.

Thus, while the Edmundite Fathers have withdrawn support of the ministries in Pine Apple and Vredenburgh, and grass-roots efforts have developed to continue there, they have turned their attention to Mosses. As outlined by the CBS program, there is certainly much to be done in Lowndes County.

Sister Kathleen Navarra has been tasked with replicating the Academy program, now two years old, in Mosses. With a median age of 37.9 years, there are many underserved youngsters in Mosses, and Sister Kathleen will be occupied with running an after-school program that will provide academic support, college and career exploration, and leadership training to junior high school students.

With the departure of Sister Nancy Clark to Rochester in 2014, Sister Janet Connorton completed the work of closing the apartment they had shared, and moved to Summerfield Road, at the site of Queen of Peace Parish. By May of that year, Sister Janet had moved back to Rochester, leaving Sisters Patricia and Kathleen to minister in Selma, Pine Apple, and Vredenburgh.

THE PAST, THE PRESENT, AND BEYOND

AFTER ALL THE UPHEAVAL, after all the legislation, after all the programs, after all the years, what is Selma today? According to Alston Fitts (2016, p. 335) "Selma is frozen in time" He quotes the Southern Poverty Law Center's *Intelligence Report:*

> *Crossing the Edmund Pettis Bridge into Selma feels like entering a time warp in which the past maintains such a stranglehold on the present that a breeze off the Alabama River seems to carry a whiff of tear gas or the distant crack of a slave master's whip.*

Indeed, a visitor to this city is at once both taken by the number of historical markers and the block after block of boarded-up, gang-tagged, derelict homes. Since the 2010 US Census, Selma lost 7% of its population in just nine years; currently it is 18,276, down from almost 23,000 ten years ago. (The population was at its peak in 1965 when it had 28,000). The statistics show that the city of Selma is 81.2% Black and it has a poverty rate of 38.3%. Twenty per cent of the residents are currently unemployed, and Selma is ranked the 71ST most dangerous city in the country. (*Citydata. com*, search January 14, 2021).

When asked, one resident remarked, "All the factories that used to be here are closed: the candy factory, the furniture company, they all picked up and moved." (*The Guardian.com/us-news, February 4, 2016, p. 5).* He continued: "Selma ain't like that movie. There everyone is shown working together and putting the past behind them. But the reality is Selma has been left behind, and folks are certainly not working together."

As of December of 2020, Sister Patricia Flass, Sister Nancy Clark, and Sister Kathleen Navarra represented the presence of the Sisters of St. Joseph of Rochester. Sister Patricia officially "retired" in 2019, but can still be found volunteering in many of the outreach projects sponsored by the Edmundites, including the Health Link and the Senior Center in Selma.

In 2019, Sister Kathleen Navarra took part in the writing of a Conrad

Hilton Foundation grant to provide for after-school tutoring, enrichment, and college and career preparation for seventh, eighth, and ninth grade students enrolled in the Selma public school and in Mosses. Having secured $500,000 from the Foundation, the Edmundites engaged Susan Raymond, a scholar with an interest in areas of poverty, to oversee the grant, leaving Sister Kathleen free to oversee and operate the Academy, described above. In addition to the academic support, this program provides speakers on various topics geared towards exposing students to various professional careers, use of computers and other learning technologies, and field trips to local colleges and universities. Currently, the Academy is housed in a renovated house contiguous to the Edmundite Center; it is dedicated to Dr. Isabelle Dumont and Miss Joan Mulder, and a picture of them hangs on the front wall of the building, thus melding the health care and teaching ministries that are the legacy of the Sisters of St. Joseph.

The grant also provides funds for the provision of opportunities in several areas of need in the more rural areas around Selma, most notably Mosses, described above, for volunteers, especially religious men and women, to come to the area. A brochure produced through the Hilton grant, geared towards attracting Sisters, describes the opportunities:

> With the support from the Catholic Sisters initiative of the Conrad N. Hilton Foundation and working with Edmundite Missions, the Sisters of St. Joseph of Rochester are developing field learning sites in three rural areas to provide congregations of Catholic sisters and lay associates in the U.S. and abroad, with the opportunity to serve the rural poor and understand how their own work might extend into rural areas...
>
> Field visits can be of any duration, but several days is optimal to understand fully the needs and the opportunity to have impact in rural settings.
>
> The goal is to provide a direct service setting where Catholic sisters can experience the importance of sponsored works addressing rural poverty. (Excerpt from a brochure produced to attract Catholic sisters, and sponsored by the Conrad N. Hilton Foundation grant, 2021).

Recently, Sisters Patricia Flass, Kathleen Navarra, and Nancy Clark sent the brochure and appeals to various religious congregations of women around the country. Much to their delight, several religious congregations have expressed interest, and a Sister from Kentucky and two Sisters from another Congregation are coming for the summer 2021 programs, and, they hope, will stay longer.

Besides all these activities, Sister Kathleen holds a fourth degree black belt in Karate. She teaches several adults and children, and regularly brings students to local, area, and national karate competitions, thus exposing students to the world outside of Selma.

As of this writing (January, 2022), Sister Nancy Clark, who had started and operated the Learning Center in Pine Apple and then in Vredenburgh for many years, returned to the area, but was in a serious auto accident in January, 2021. She had planned to help Sister Kathleen Navarra with the requirements of the Hilton Grant by contacting various institutions of higher learning to arrange visits for the students in the Academy. However, in March, 2021, she returned to Rochester to stay because her injuries from the accident would prevent her from tending to her responsibilities.

How does one assess the many years of the Sisters' presence in Selma and the surroundings?

> *What happens to a dream deferred?*
> *Does it dry up like a raisin in the sun?*
> *Or fester like a sore-and then run?*
> *Does it stink like rotten meat?*
> *Or crust and sugar over—*
> *Like a syrupy sweet?*
> *Maybe it just sags like a heavy load.*
> *Or does it explode?*
>
> *- Langston Hughes, Harlem, 1951*

In the case of Selma, the dream has "sag[ged] like a heavy load". The optimism that reigned in the 1960's has been tempered by the fact that economic sustainability has largely passed by Selma, just like the interstate highways. Today, the entire City government is Black, starting with Mayor James Perkins, son of Good Samaritan alumna, Etta Perkins. The police chief is a Black man and the schools superintendent is Black. Private business is doing its part to revitalize the city and visitors can now have brunch in the newly opened St. James Hotel, and then stroll through the Selma Interpretive Center, or the National Voting Rights Museum or any of a multitude of sites dedicated to the struggle for civil rights. One detects a strong whiff of nostalgia in Selma as a tourist map directs visitors to numerous civil rights landmarks. Chris Arnade, in a 2016 article for the *Guardian*, quotes a Selma resident: "We never harm tourists. Never. Got that. We keep our [stuff] to ourselves. They come here because special things DID happen here. Just wish they would happen again." (*February 4, 2016, p. 12*).

In his essay, *The Hottest Place in Hell (2015)* Gregory Hite observed what happened after the excitement of the Selma to Montgomery marches:

> When the marchers and the television cameras left town, the priests, nuns, and parishioners at St. Elizabeth's went back to the job of running the mission, the school, and the hospital. Divine protection, Father Ouellet noted, was 'more necessary now than ever. We're almost certain to be the main targets for reprisal and hatred from some elements in the white community for what happened in Selma these past three weeks. There are always crackpots. Our lives are in danger and we know it.' However, what truly concerned him was that the nation would believe that the battle for equal rights had been won in Selma.

In a 2021 interview, Mayor Perkins, recently elected to a third term, noted: "Selma has done more for the world than the world has done for Selma." He cited the need to find funds to fix the many and serious problems endemic to Selma. "If we can train the women, the women will turn the men around. The men need to take responsibility as fathers. We are starting to eradicate the gangs here, and we are starting to address the problem of educating our youth." (Interview with Mayor James Perkins, February 12, 2021). Interestingly, how prescient was Sister Frances Marie when she remarked: "the salvation of Selma lies in the moral uplifting of its women." It should be remembered, too, that the Good Samaritan nursing school had been geared towards empowering and enabling women; the Sisters had always kept their eyes on this endeavor.

Thankfully, Mayor Perkins has an optimistic outlook, and, as he remarked, " I am ready to roll up my sleeves to get the work done." He related that he has traveled to Korea twice to entice the Kia automobile manufacturing company to bring an auto parts plant to Selma; that is still in the offing. During his first two terms (2000-2004, 2004-2008), the mayor tried to take on the school system, which, to say the least, has let down the young people of Selma. He lost that fight, but, with a new schools superintendent, sees a path to serious improvement in the education offered to Selma's youth.

The post civil rights era, in many ways, reflects the time of Reconstruction after the Civil War. The headiness that infected all in the immediate aftermath has settled into a series of struggles that seek to address issues once thought of as settled. Trillions of dollars have gone into improvement programs since President Lyndon Johnson affirmed the New Society, and yet, one still sees, in central Alabama, vast inequities in education, employment, and housing. Misbegotten legislation and welfare programs have eroded Black nuclear families; the education system has failed to train Black children in the skills needed to thread their way through self-sufficiency, and recent events have eroded trust in the political and judicial systems.

Investments in Black businesses have been sorely lacking. Programs intended to last a short time to "get people back on their feet" have created generations of people dependent on government, making poor people wards of the State.

Although the COVID 19 pandemic has barred residents from gathering at the Edmundite Center for the nightly meal, the Center staff prepares several hundred meals to be picked up nightly. The number of meals is a testament to the continued need for basics in Selma. The many senior citizens in Selma used to gather on Thursday afternoons at the Edmundite Center for cake, cards and conversation. Unfortunately, that ritual is on hold as of this writing, and, once again, seniors are home-bound.

Sister Kathleen Navarra fondly remembers a couple from Bergin, New

York, who traveled to Pine Apple every summer:

> *Don and Pat Burke had retired early from their jobs in Roch-*
> *ester. They bought a recreational vehicle and drove it to Pine Ap-*
> *ple every summer. They volunteered in the summer program and*
> *generally helped out wherever they saw the need. They would cook*
> *barbeques for everyone and everybody looked forward to their ar-*
> *rival. When the grandchildren demanded their attention and they*
> *stopped coming down, they donated the recreational vehicle so that*
> *volunteers had a place to stay and medical students interning with*
> *Sister Roseann in the clinic had a place to sleep. (Interview with*
> *Sister Kathleen Navarra, March 17, 2021).*

But how does one evaluate the four score of presence and work of the Sisters of St. Joseph in central Alabama? Where does one start?

Having queried the Sisters currently living and working in Selma (Sisters Patricia Flass, and Kathleen Navarra), this is their response.

> *The local people could take over the leadership and operation*
> *of the programs that have been begun. There are examples of that*
> *in Pine Apple and Vredenburgh. There are so few Sisters left at all,*
> *but scores of young people have traveled to this area as volunteers;*
> *maybe some of them will get involved in these ministries.*
>
> *As one of the employees of the Edmundites has remarked: 'the*
> *Edmundites raise the money and the Sisters do all the work'. To*
> *which might be added, the Edmundites had the vision and grit to*
> *found the Alabama missions and to fund them. It was the Sisters*
> *who went out to the rural areas and started various ministries to*
> *meet those unique needs, but they always had the support and the*
> *admiration of the Edmundite Fathers. Many religious congrega-*
> *tions' Sisters were here doing a multitude of tasks. Now there are*
> *only three. (Sister Patricia, Sister Kathleen Navarra, Sister Jane*
> *Kelley, CSJ)*
>
> *We are concerned that the ministries have taken on more of a*
> *business model: exigencies of the finances of the Edmundites and*
> *of the economy in general have made taking on new projects a real*
> *challenge.*

We plan to stay as long was we can; after that we really don't have any control.

Indeed, the Edmundites have pulled out of the projects that were planted so many years ago in Pine Apple and Vrededburgh, but there, either local government or local people have taken over the previous projects. Perhaps the real mark of the mission has been the involvement of the people themselves. For example, Mary's Food and Fashion, the snack and clothing shop, is now operated by a group called Partners in Progress. The major support is from a Black church and is directed by Doris Smith, who originally worked with Sister Mary Maloy. Although Sister Kathleen Navarra oversees projects in Vredenburgh, much of the support there has come from Prince of Peace Parish in Birmingham, Alabama, and a group called Building a Better Community, who built the multi-use building that stands as a testament to their generosity. In addition to the monetary donations, in-kind labor put the finishing touches on this much-used facility. Sister Kathleen Navarra explains how this was accomplished:

We were looking for funds to build during the depths of the 2008 recession. We decided that we did not want to ask for money from businesses, but from individuals, and so we approached people in Birmingham. They came up with about $200,000, and local residents in Vredenburgh donated their time and supplies to finish off the building. It was a point of pride for everyone that we got a $400,000 facility for half of that. (Interview with Sister Kathleen Navarra, March 17, 2021).

There are plans to begin some projects in nearby Mosses, including an academy for the junior high school students modeled on that in Selma, and Sister Kathleen would be overseeing the Academy project in both places. But, in 2021, most of the work is centered in Selma. In 2020 the Bullock Community and Recreation Center was completed. It is a modern building with a gym, exercise areas and meeting rooms and stands just across Broad Street from the convent that the Sisters occupied in 1940. The project was financed by the Edmundite Fathers and generous donors, and testifies to the staying power of the Church in Selma, and the continued support of the Edmundite vision.

The Edmundite Center of Hope, further down Broad Street, has also been renovated to provide examining rooms and facilities for the health initiative, and, of course, the meal program continues.

When the current Sisters try to determine what needs to happen next, Sister Nancy Clark relates two stories:

> *Bishop Lipscomb had visited Pine Apple in 2000 and told us 'try to build bridges with the white people; cultivate the white people.' So we attended fundraisers and other events that had white people to let them see that we were all for the same goals.*
>
> *Sister Mary Maloy and I went to Montgomery in 1990 to attend the thirty-fifth celebration of 'Bloody Sunday', and we spotted Coretta Scott King. We made our way over to her and introduced ourselves, and told her that our Sisters had been here for fifty years. She told us: 'go to the white people; build a bridge with the white people and see what you can do with them. The Black people can't do this without the white people.' (Interview with Sister Nancy Clark, March 7, 2021)*

In 1940, the Sisters had been considered "Black" because they worked exclusively with the Black people of Selma. They had endured the vitriol and odium that had been suffered by Black people for a century, and, at times put their lives in danger. The eighty years that followed, in a residual racism that endures to this day, found the Sisters working in spite of the white people and not with them. Eighty years later, they were encouraged to build bridges with the white community.

In many ways, to this day, the people of the Southern United States carry the onus of their forebears. The current mavens of culture would wish to eradicate the events of the past, but the past is the past; pretty or ugly, events happened. Stereotypes should not blind people to see only black and white; there are plenty of shades and nuances to be found.

The Sisters of St. Joseph were tasked with figuring out what people needed, and with designing structures and methods to meet those needs. For the first twenty-five years, they pretty much stayed out of the political struggles and efforts at equality. But that is not to say that they did not see the injustices all around them. Instead, they quietly and characteristically got to work.

After the events of March, 1965, they took a more active role, as did many religious men and women, and, eventually, the hierarchical Church. However, the dialectic still prevails. The future lies in the melding of human aspirations, and the enabling of people, Black and white, to see that human aspirations have so much in common.

Perhaps in response to the question of how to evaluate the eighty years of Sisters' presence, Sister Mary Maloy, in her 1990 reflection, sums up the experience of so many Sisters of St. Joseph who labored in the Alabama missions in Selma and beyond:

I had hoped to come to some understanding, there, in Alabama. I had hoped to gain some insight, to grasp some elusive truth, to come to some truce in the inner war. It didn't happen; it only defined more battlefields, showed me new theaters of struggle.

And I never did cast my lot among them, not really. I have, of them, only a bittersweet memory of a country church alive with faith and passion; of shy children living without stimulation of light or color, whose world is surrounded by dirt road and deep wood, children loved and controlled by adults who want them to "be sweet, now" but cannot understand the longings of their hearts; of families living for generations on the same land; of sons and daughters returned from the north to their quiet roots, belonging nowhere restless, frustrated and have, of me, nothing. For I had nothing to give, nothing but admiration and apology and thanks for letting me in for awhile. (SSJ Archives)

Sisters of St. Joseph of Rochester Who Served in Alabama 1940-2020

Sr. Agnes Therese Gundy

Sr. Albertine Devereaux

Sr. Alma Joseph Bauman

Sr. Alonzo Bulanda

Sr. Anastasia McCormick

Sr. Anita Kurowski

Sr. Angelia Dear

Sr. Angeline McCann

Sr. Anna Patricia Barry

Sr. Anne Hyland

Sr. Anne Urquhart

Sr. Anne Maura Morris

Sr. Barbara Lum

Sr. Barbara Olmstead

Sr. Basil Minch

Sr. Catherine Gibbons

Sr. Catherine Charlotte Hyland

Sr. Catherine Teresa Martin

Sr. Francis David Backman

Sr. Frances Marie Kehoe

Sr. Francis de Sales Murphy

Sr. Francis Mary Rossi

Sr. Francis Xavier Dailor

Sr. Grace Noel Gleichauf

Sr. Gregory Carroll

Sr. Hilary Hanly

Sr. Isabel Fitzgerald

Sr. James Eileen Kavanaugh

Sr. Janet Connorton

Sr. Joan Marshall

Sr. Joan Francis Hauser

Sr. Joseph Anne Collins

Sr. Christine Wagner

Sr. Christine Francis Saldanha

Sr. Christine Regina Englert

Sr. Clare Torpey

Sr. Colette Holland

Sr. Concepta Vay

Sr. Cyril Smelt

Sr. Dolores Bachman

Sr. Dominic Burke

Sr. Domitilla Leicht

Sr. Dorothy Quinn

Sr. Dorothy Ellen Muldoon

Sr. Doretta Rhodes

Sr. Eleanor Chilbert

Sr. Electa Spada

Sr. Evangelist Ryan

Sr. Evelyn Connolly

Sr. Florentine McCarthy

Sr. Kathleen Fletcher

Sr. Kathleen Navarra

Sr. Katrina Amos

Sr. Liguori Dunlea

Sr. Lois Riley

Sr. Loretta Poole

Sr. Lorraine Julien

Sr. Louis Bertrand Dixon

Sr. Loyola Guider

Sr. Lucina Flaherty

Sr. Margaret Kunder

Sr. Margaret Isabelle Tracy

Sr. Margaretta MacCarthy

Sr. Marie Albert Alderman

Sr. Joseph Clare Kent

Sr. Josepha Twomey

Sr. Josephine Collins

Sr. Josette Capozzi

Sr. Marilyn Pray

Sr. Marlene Pape

Sr. Martha Gersbach

Sr. Mary Colgan

Sr. Mary Maloy

Sr. Mary Scollan

Sr. Mary Weaver

Sr. Mary Ann Brunett

Sr. Mary Christopher Kuchman

Sr. Mary Denis Hurley

Sr. Mary Ellen Dundon

Sr. Mary Jane Mitchell

Sr. Mary Louise Mitchell

Sr. Mary Paul Geck

Sr. Mary Roch Basso

Sr. Maureen Finn

Sr. Michael Ann Hanly

Sr. Nancy Clark

Sr. Helen Norwood

Sr. Marie Therese Warth

Sr. Margaret Adelaide Owen

Sr. Marelise McCarrick

Sr. Patricia Flass

Sr. Patricia McDermott

Sr. Paul Marie Dougherty

Sr. Philomena DeSocio

Sr. Remigia McHenry

Sr. Rita Quigley

Sr. Rose Frisk

Sr. Rose Margaret Marconi

Sr. St. Joseph Creighton

Sr. Sharon Bailey

Sr. Shirley Casler

Sr. Sienna Cameron

Sr. Uriel Vernetti

Sr. Vincent Joseph Miles

Sr. Vincentine Broderick

Sr. Virginia Mahaney

Sr. Wilhelmina Martin

To these women and to all who have labored in the vineyard of the Lord, the Church owes an inestimable gift of gratitude.

SOURCES

1. Archives of the Sisters of St. Joseph of Rochester; these include letters, annals, meting minutes, and recorded archives, 1940-2020.
2. Arnade, C. (2016). Still a city of slaves: Selma in the words of those who live there. *The Guardian.* Http://theguardian.com/us-news/2016/feb/04.
3. Benn, A. Two brothers pay $75,000 for hospital. (July 2, 1984) *Montgomery(AL) Messenger.*
4. Brinckman, J. (May, 1958). *More than a good Samaritan.* The Colored Harvest, Josephite Missionaries, 12-14.
5. Bryan, H. (2016). Selma works to resurrect hospital known as 'Good Sam'. WSFA Channel 12 News.
6. City-Data.com., record search May 21, 2021.
7. Coburn, C. & Smith, M. (1999). *Spirited lives: how nuns shaped Catholic culture and American life, 1836-1920.* University of North Carolina Press, Chapel Hill, NC.
8. Dream realized. *Selma Times Journal,* November 22, 1964.
9. Fitts, A. (1985, August). A sign of hope in Selma. St. Anthony Messenger. 29-31.
10. Fitts, A. (2016) *Selma; a bicentennial history.* University of Alabama Press, Tuscaloosa, AL.
11. Fitts, A. Selma has lost a saint.(May 24, 1985). *The Catholic Week,* 1.
12. Garrison, G. 2018. Alabama's iconic civil right town now the fastest shrinking city in the state. Http://www.al.com/news/2018/12/alabamas -iconic civil rights town.
13. Gordon, T. (1985, November 21). Joan Mulder's life was one of love for others. *Birmingham (AL)News,*
14. History of Our Lady Queen of Peace Parish in Selma: 1850-2015. Bulletin of Our Lady Queen of Peace Parish.
15. Hite, G. (2002) The hottest places in hell: The Catholic Church and civil rights in Selma, Alabama 1937-1965. Dissertation in satisfaction of Doctor of Theology, University of Virginia.
16. Know your fine diocesan schools. (September 26, 1975) *The Catholic Week.*
17. Missions all encompassing. (1975, May 7). *Rochester Catholic Courier-Journal.*
18. Nolan, C. Selma then-the world now: A visit to the Edmund Pettis Bridge and justice today. March 9, 2015.1-4. Http://globalsistersreport.org.

19. SSJ's mark 35th anniversary of bloody Sunday (2000, Summer) *The Bridge, Newsletter of the Sisters of St. Joseph of Rochester.*

20. Shaw, D.L. Sixty years of sisterhood. *Finger Lakes Times*, October 7, 2007.

21. Sikora, F. (1985, May). Selma doctor to buried with blacks she aided.

22. *Birmingham (AL) News.*

23. Traxler, M.M. *Collected writings 1970-1992.* Marquette University Collection.

24. Walburn, J. (1984, July 1) Good Sam sold. *Selma Times-Journal.*

25. Wallis, J. (2015). Selma and our next bridge to cross. *Sojourners. Http://sojo.net/print/blogs/2015/03/12/selma-and-our-next-bridge-cross.*

26. Wall, BM. (2009). *Catholic sister nurses in Selma, Alabama, 1940-1972.* Author manuscript in satisfaction of Ph.D., University of Pennsylvania School of Nursing, Philadelphia, PA.

27. Weinblatt, T. (2016) An analysis of the success of the civil rights movement. University of Maryland Honors Undergraduate Paper.

About the Author

Carol Cimino, SSJ, Ed.D. is a Sister of St. Joseph of Rochester. She is a life-long educator and has served as a teacher, a development director, a director for a state-wide Catholic school administrators' association and an administrator in Catholic schools since 1965. She has authored several books and articles for Catholic publications. She retired as the superintendent of Catholic schools in the Diocese of Buffalo, NY in 2018. However, she continues to serve as an associate professor at Manhattan College, a national consultant for the Wm. H. Sadlier publishing company, and a consultant for Catholic School Management, Inc. She is, perhaps, proudest of the fact that she is still the only religious sister to have been a 3-day champion on "Jeopardy!"

Made in United States
Orlando, FL
12 June 2022